TOUCHSTONE

LINDA EATMON-JONES

Outskirts Press, Inc.
http://www.outskirtspress.com

ISBN: 978-1-4787-7309-2

Outskirts Press and the "OP" logo are trademarks belonging to Outskirts Press, Inc.

PRINTED IN THE UNITED STATES OF AMERICA

DENVER, COLORADO

Dedicated to:

Our Grandkids

Ryan and Rachael Eatmon

Our Great-Nephews

Paul, Samuel and Alexandre Delevoye

"GREATEST" GREAT-UNCLE   QUIET SERVANT

THE BEST ROLE MODEL   HUMBLE MAN   A THINKER

EARLE "THE TOUCHSTONE" JONES

THE LITTLE BROTHER WHO'S MORE THAN "LITTLE"

FAITHFUL FATHER AND DEVOTED GRANDFATHER

SAVED, SURRENDERED, AND SERVING

REAL DEAL EARLE   A RIGHTEOUS BROTHER

EARLE FRANCIS JONES

Essays of His Works and Service

ALWAYS A SMILE WITH THANKS   AMAZING FRIEND

COOL, CARING DUDE   THE NICEST NEPHEW EVER

THE EARL(E) OF JONES   WISE COUNSELOR, MENTOR, AND FRIEND

"COMCAST CARES" GIVER   NO ORDINARY MAN

"READY, STEADY" EARLE JONES   THE FLUTE PLAYER

MY OLDER BROTHER/BRO-N-LAW

THE GENTLE GIANT'S BIG HEART WITH FAMOUS FRIENDS

JUST EARLE   GREAT SECTION II CLASSMATE

THE GENTLE GIANT'S BIG HEART   THE RIGHT MAN FOR MY NEPHEW

A CHRISTIAN BROTHER AND FAMILY MAN

EARLE JONES, MY COLLEAGUE & MY FRIEND

THE FAMILY UNIFIER   LOYAL FRIEND   THE MENTEE MENTORS

A GRACIOUS MAN   A GENUINE NICE GUY

HUMILITY, JOY, SINCERITY, AND FAITH   CAPTAIN EARLE

WHO IS UNCLE EARLE?   TELECOM POLICY EXTRAORDINAIRE

COOL, CALM, AND COLLECTED   THE BIG MAN'S HEART

A MAN OF ALL SEASONS   ALWAYS A GENTLEMAN

VOICE OF CALM AND REASON   REDISCOVERED CLASSMATE

MY PERSONAL CHAMPION   MODERN-DAY ATLAS

A MAN OF CARING, SERVICE, AND CONVICTION

EXECUTIVE GIVING BACK   UNCLE EARLE, THE MAN WHO . . .

BOALT HALL'S DANCING MACHINE   SUPERMAN-IN-WAITING

"BROTHER EARLE," THE EPITOME OF NOBILITY

In Loving Memory of Earle's Parents

Earle and Sylvia Jones

Wedding Day 1942

TABLE OF CONTENTS

FOREWORD

By R. Donahue (Don) Peebles
Real Estate Developer

In the book *Touchstone,* the author, Linda Eatmon-Jones, provides an invaluable insight into how Earle F. Jones's legacy impacted the man we have come to know. Most importantly, that legacy taught Earle how to teach others the importance of: a strong and consistent commitment to education; acquisition of knowledge; community service; honor to country; motivation and confidence to spread your wings to soar; faith in God; courage to face adversity and move through it; and, being your brother's keeper.

The chapter outlining the horrendous loss his grandparents suffered in Georgia is compelling. His grandfather took the time to teach him lessons on how to overcome adversity and successfully move ahead and expected each to pass those lessons on to succeeding generations.

While Earle knows and works daily with influential people such as congressional members, executives in private and public sectors, on boards, foundations, and associations, he never forgets his fellow man. His community service is selfless, as described by many who wrote essays for the book.

Earle's senior executives and work colleagues acknowledge in their essays the important role he played in the successes of organizations and corporations where he's worked and continues to work in both Denver and the metro DC area. His friends' essays speak to his rock steadiness as a friend and the joy he brings to the relationship. Earle is a man of deep faith, as witnessed in the essays from his church friends. His devotion, dedication, and overall respect for people are seen as a hallmark of the man he is.

Throughout the book, you find countless examples of Earle taking the time to mentor in all aspects of a person's life, serve selflessly at church, work on community boards, and volunteer where needed in both his career and community. Thorough all this, he spends quality time with family and his precious grandkids.

As we are taught in the book of Proverbs, "Wisdom resides in the heart of the discerning and truly wise gentleman." Earle Jones became that wise gentleman through his life experiences, as documented by his wife, Linda. He is truly a *"Touchstone"* for all.

ACKNOWLEDGMENTS

★ To my Heavenly Father, Jesus said, "He is the vine and we are the branch, and without Him, we can do nothing" (John 15:5). The ideas and thoughts that came to me when I got stuck and tired came from that "vine" feeding my "branch."

★ My gratitude and deepest appreciation to the essay contributors who put my requests for input, the infamous "Essay," ahead of the many things they had going on in their very busy lives. They used the format I provided without question or concern so there could be consistency of input. There could be no book without their essays. They were also a source of positive support and inspiration during my journey. At the end, there were 88 essays of input—way more than I dreamed I could collect for my first book. Thank you, thank you.

★ I am truly blessed and thankful to have a caring, committed circle of friends and family. They have given me invaluable suggestions, comments, and support. I listened closely to their words as they each possess great wisdom and insight.

★ Sylvia Jones Turrell, my sister-in-law (actually, my older sister), provided me facts on the Jones and Carroll family history and on Earle's early days growing up. Her feedback was invaluable—the ultimate cheerleader you need on the sidelines of your race.

★ Terri Watts, my cousin and publisher of three books, provided me invaluable "book writing" guidance, inspiration to "just do it, cous," and finding me a publisher.

★ Steve and Heather Eatmon, my son and daughter-in-law, they always believe I can do anything—so they just acted like I could. Their encouragement was simply they believed I could, no matter the obstacles; Mom, always finds a way. I am very grateful for the confidence you continue to have in me and the love and support you show me each day.

★ Abby Taylor and Helen Latten were my primary manuscript readers and provided the best of their knowledge and professional experience. Each is a credentialed educator. Thank you, my sisters in Christ.

★ My deepest appreciation to Phyllis Blair and "Spyke" Henry for contacting a significant number of Earle's Coolidge High School classmates and getting their input for essays.

★ Rene Rambo-Rodgers provided me information on other law school colleagues that knew Earle, which then connected me with Milele Archibald. Milele sent me all the old photos of law school classmates she had maintained over the years and the inside joke about the "bump." So grateful for your support, and I do owe you.

★ Joshua Rich's lyrics and musical arrangement captured Earle's life in song. His overall eye for seeing how to represent Earle's life works and service in an artistic manner—many thanks.

★ My appreciation to Bret Perkins, whose essay of Earle "Touchstone" Jones prompted the idea to use *"Touchstone"* as the book's title and Joshua Rich for pointing it out.

★ Wiley Daniel gave me invaluable insight and information on the years Earle spent in Denver and took the time to help me reach out to others in Denver that knew Earle during those days.

★ My dearest Earle for being the kind of person he is—trusting and not a snoop—he respects your privacy and generally just does not bother to look at what you're doing unless he's ask you to do something for him—it allowed me many opportunities to work on the book while we were even talking at the kitchen counter. Thank you for being you.

INTRODUCTION

Many years ago, I was sitting in my hometown church in North Carolina at my father's funeral fiddling with the program as a means of distraction from my overwhelming grief. I started to read it and saw that his best friend, Mr. John Sessoms, would sing one of my father's favorite songs to honor him. They sang together in a men's chorus for many years, traveling around the east coast of North Carolina. This was one of the songs where my father sang the lead.

I saw the program while it was being created and even helped to develop some of it, but did not notice the title of the song Mr. Sessoms would sing in my father's honor, which was "May the Works I've Done Speak for Me." As Mr. Sessoms began the song, I looked around the church—so many people—crowded in the balcony, the lobby, every seat in the church filled, with chairs on each aisle. It dawned on me—the people here represented the "works" that were silently speaking on behalf of my father.

When I started on this journey to give tribute to Earle F. Jones's life works and service, I could not get that song out of my head. The words are so simple but so powerful— *"May the works I've done speak for me. May the service I provide speak for me. May the life I live speak for me."* Earle's life story is in the works he does, the service he provides, and the life he lives. I knew the book structure would be fairly straightforward— Earle's works and service speaking for him or what they represent in the lives of the people he touched . . . hence, the title *Touchstone.*

I met Earle through a friend of mine from grade school. He had known Earle for over 15 years in Denver, Colorado, and clearly knew me. I was divorced with a teen son and was not really looking to marry again anytime soon—my work life and raising a son as a single parent was about all I could handle. However, my friend persisted, and I agreed, for him to give Earle my phone number. Even when my friend gave Earle my phone number, I was away in Boston working on an executive MBA through my job and had 2 more months left on campus before I could return to my home in the DC area. Earle waited for me to return to meet me. That was when I thought, he must be a pretty special guy. We met for lunch, and the rest is history.

I found out after 20-some years that he was *really* a special guy, so I decided to author a biography of Earle's life, including many short essays from those who knew him in a particular area in his life. Who better to tell the story of the works and service of this incredible man whose humility limits even his thoughts of writing an autobiography of his outstanding life. The biography pulls together in one place the many facets of his life presented through small essays authored by family, friends, and colleagues weaved through my descriptions of the road he's traveled.

If you were to ask Earle about his life just to get a general sense of who he is, what he's done, and where he's been, you'd probably get this response: "I'm a native of Washington, DC, and received my undergraduate degree from The American University and my Juris Doctorate from the University of California, Berkeley School of Law. I've worked in the cable industry for over 25 years. I've served on the board of directors of a number of organizations, including: the Congressional Black Caucus Foundation, the Greater Washington

Urban League, and Smart Activities for Fitness and Education (SAFE)." These are the exact words he provides when asked for biographical information. Brief, truthful, succinct, and to the point; however, there is so much more to Earle's life that I will attempt to describe and share in this book with the input from so many essay writers.

Earle has a compelling life story that *he* should hear, and it is also an inspiration to others. I think of Earle's life as a pie that has already been sliced and served on separate plates, being enjoyed by many involved in a slice without seeing the whole pie. One group's interaction may be through the slice of his professional career in the cable industry, the slice of community service, while another through the slice of boards, foundations, and fraternities, another through the slice of his church involvement, the slice of family—father, father-in-law, granddad, brother, niece, son-in-law, uncle, brother-in-law, cousin, nephew, and the slice of a dear friend for life, and so on.

As his wife, I get to see the whole pie every day and have admired Earle's commitment and dedication to each slice and his personal interactions that provides respect and regard to all. I am able to see his determination to provide the same level of thoroughness and thoughtfulness to an agenda for a community service meeting or for a meeting for senior executives at his job or congressmen on Capitol Hill. He always returns phone calls, e-mails, and text messages promptly and courteously—he doesn't tweet J, but if he did, you'd get a prompt tweet from him.

Many people know Earle in multiple slices. Several of his relationships might have started out as a professional one at work or in business endeavors, then moved into a lasting friendship because of shared personal values. In those instances, the primary area of their interaction is where most wrote their essays; however, in almost every one of those instances, each acknowledges the deep friendship and admiration they feel for Earle.

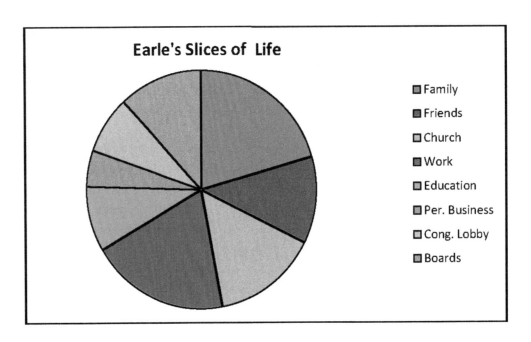

After developing the slices, I was struck by how balanced they were. Family is the largest slice with friends and church about equal, and education (reading, traveling, or the acquisition of knowledge) being a tad bit smaller. His professional work includes the time spent at Comcast and volunteer boards, foundations, and associations. However, collectively, they are not greater than family, friends, church, and education.

My goal was to gather the works and service within each slice and let them speak for him throughout his life, representing significant milestones of his life and its impact on him and others. I categorized his works and service into eight slices and provide a description of each area, Earle's role, what the areas mean to him, and how he has embodied his beliefs in those areas. Small essays written by the people who are/were the closest to Earle describe those individuals' interactions with Earle in this slice of his life.

I feel it is important that we pay tribute and provide our praises and honor to people while the person can still read them and not need someone to read to them or read over them. With this book, I am taking the opportunity to honor Earle with written expressions of the respect, admiration, and love from the many people he has touched. For over 5 decades, Earle has given of himself with humility and service to others, with little regard for himself. He has never sought public acclaim for his works or service. He does things for the right reasons—to serve others and God.

I looked up the name Earle on "Behind the Name" to get a sense of what the name means and if his life fits his name. His first name is the same as his father's, which is not unusual for a father to name his son after him. The words used to describe Earle seem so fitting to the man I came to know—masculine, classic, mature, formal, wholesome, strong, intellectual, serious, courageous, but also kindhearted, dependable, supportive, caring, and sensitive to the needs of others. Perhaps there was some wisdom in what his father saw in him from day one.

Being married to Earle brings other distinguished and humorous moments. In our travels, I am often amazed by the number of people who mistake Earle for *James Earl Jones* or *Colin Powell*. Case in point, at the 2016 Presidential Debate in Charleston, SC, a young man working to help a secret service agent check and verify IDs for entrance, posts this in a blog he wrote afterward displaying the "selfies" he took with "celebrities and congressmen," which included a "selfie" of him and Earle. Louis Shenker, from Longmeadow, Massachusetts, says in his blog post, "We then proceeded to check the IDs of the congressmen and celebrities entering the back against the names printed on their ticket. This is when I met James Earl Jones (the voice of Darth Vader and Mufasa), and I asked him to take a picture because I'm a big fan of him."

Earle always complies, even when he tells the person he is not that person—they think he is trying to fly under the radar, and they give him a "wink and a nod," as to say, "I'm not going to blow your cover." Whether it's getting on a plane, hailing a taxi, entering a professional event, or checking into a hotel, it is truly astonishing how many times he is stopped. He's always that same selfless Earle, just smiling or nodding or making some general comment to the person.

Most have heard the old cliché, "it's not where you come from, but it's where you're going" to let people know they are not limited by one's upbringing, their past, or choices made in life. However, in Earle's instance, I think it's the reverse—**where he came from definitely shaped where he went and molded the person he is today.**

My hope is Earle's life story and his legacy provide the inspiration for anyone in any stage of their life to realize that your thoughts create beliefs, beliefs create attitudes, attitudes create behaviors, and behaviors create results. Your values and principles drive your thought—from there, you set the limit. Others will sing your praises!!

NEW DAY...NEW PLACE...NEW BEGINNING

It is said that history repeats itself, but we are only doomed to relive our past if we fail to learn from it. The past is not a map to where you are going; it's a record of where you have been. Its purpose is not to drag you back through emotional muck, but to serve you best by reminding you of lessons learned so you can avoid them in the future. ~from React or Respond by Kimberly and Tom Goodwin

Earle's paternal grandfather and grandmother were Samuel and Nettie Jones. They had four children: Earle's father, whose name was also Earle (whom I will refer to as Earle Sr.) and who was the oldest, two daughters, Evelyn and Mildred, and the youngest son, Karl. The family lived in Sylvester, Georgia, from the early 1900s until an extremely horrifying and senseless act occurred around 1921. The Ku Klux Klan (KKK) burned to the ground all their property, belongings, and family heirlooms. By the grace of God, the family was not injured and escaped to Jacksonville, Florida. They never knew why they were targeted for a KKK raid.

For a year, the family stayed in Florida with relatives while Sam Jones went to Philadelphia, Pa., to look for a place to move his family so they could start over again. Earle Sr. was 7, Evelyn and Mildred were 5 and 3, respectively, and Karl was the baby. Sam was determined not to let this traumatic event define the family's future.

Sam learned how to read and taught his older children, nieces, and nephews to read also. He constantly talked about the importance of education and why it was needed in one's life. Sam took on odd jobs during that year, and it was really tough because these were the early days of the Great Depression. However, Sam was able to save enough money to purchase fares for the family to actually be stowaways on a Portuguese steam engine ship traveling north.

Earle Sr. fondly remembers the flying fish in the Atlantic Ocean, when they could come up on deck. One cannot imagine the strength and courage it took for the family to leave their roots in Georgia without anything, and then leave family in Florida—all this within 1 year of such a devastating time. The path Sam Jones took not only saved his family but taught them a powerful lesson on *moving ahead without anger* and *not let it consume or stop you from doing better*.

Once the ship's captain dropped them off in Philadelphia, Sam again took on odd jobs he saw when he visited the year earlier. Because he could read, he was able to find enough work to feed his family and save a little. In a short time, he had enough money to move his family to Newtonville, New Jersey, where he could farm as a sharecropper and put the kids in school.

Earle Sr. started school at Vineland Elementary at the age of 8 and was put in the third grade. He had never been in a school before and had missed the first two grades that all the other kids had gone through. Neither Sam nor Nettie complained. Another example of taking the hand you are dealt and making the best decisions you can to continue to move forward. Earle Sr. was the only black in the elementary school. It was not long before he caught up and academically passed the other kids in his classes. From elementary through high school graduation, Earle Sr. was always in the highest achiever group making almost all *As*. We still have some of his report cards from those years. Another lesson from Sam to his children—*Do not let the situation define you—you define it.*

In the late 1920s, Sam Jones was able to purchase property in Newtonville, N.J., where he continued to farm, but on his own farm, until the late 1930s. He continued into his senior years to stress the importance of education. He had children and grandchildren graduating from college in the '40s, '50s, and '60s, when many blacks were not graduating from high school. Another lesson . . . *"Give a man a fish and you feed him for a day; teach a man to fish and you feed him for a lifetime". ~ Maimonides*

Despite graduating high school during the Great Depression, Earle Sr. established several firsts: he was in the first group of young men enlisted in the newly created CCCs (Civil Conservation Corps), where he worked with distinction for 5 years on public works projects in the states of New York, Virginia, and Montana—another form of education through traveling. After receiving a bachelor's degree from Trenton Teachers College, now named College of New Jersey, he was one of the first African Americans to work in the Social Security Administration in Baltimore in 1939. Serving in the U.S. Navy during World War II, he was stationed in the Pacific from 1944 to the end of the war. Another lesson—*Serve your country, and it will serve you.*

Earle Sr. used the GI bill to obtain an additional bachelor's and a master's degree in physics and belonged to the Sigma Pi Sigma honor society at Howard University in Washington, DC. He was one of the first African Americans on the research staff in the Sound Section of the National Bureau of Standards. Earle Sr. was also one of the first African American fellows elected into the National Acoustical Society, which was primarily white at the time. He coauthored over a dozen research articles that were published in various national journals from 1952–1967, including the Acoustical Society of America. He helped found the Science and Engineering Club to unite minority physicists in the DC area. Another lesson—*Lift up your fellow man.*

The DC community service of Earle Sr. included forming the first Block Association with the police department and the Maxi Arts Gala in collaboration with DC public schools. He was an active member of Alpha Phi Alpha fraternity at Howard University. The Maxi Arts Gala featured great local African American circus performers. The Caroling for Children program for Children's Hospital was another project he initiated. Both of these programs lasted over 20 years and were widely known and supported by the DC communities. Earle Sr. often appeared on local TV stations, promoting his programs. Another lesson—*Community work pays off.*

Earle Sr. married the former Sylvia Carroll in 1942 in Washington, DC, and from that union of 54 years were born Sylvia Elaine and Earle Francis (Earle Sr. did not have a middle name; hence, Earle was not a junior). They were fondly called Little Sylvia and Little Earle, even though Little Earle grew to be 6 foot 3—over 7 inches taller than his father, Earle Sr. Both Little Sylvia and Little Earle attended elementary through high school and undergraduate colleges in DC, with each moving away for postgraduate education.

Earle's mother graduated in 1937 from Miner Teacher's College in DC, which was later merged into the University of the District of Columbia. She received a master's degree in English literature from Howard University. She was a second-generation college graduate—her mother, Mable O. Carroll, graduated from Howard University in 1917 and taught school in DC and Wilmington, Delaware. Her family used the same path to success as Sam Jones established as a legacy for his family—stressing the importance of education to young people.

A passionate educator of history, English, and literature, she taught at Morris College, Sumter, S.C., from 1937 to 1939, in the Baltimore school system from 1939 to 1942, and for 40 years in the Washington, DC, school system where she taught at Garnet Patterson Jr. High (1949 to 1985).

Sylvia Jones was always heavily involved in civic affairs, devoting her time to dozens of organizations, especially for causes related to children and young people. She assumed numerous responsibilities including: founder and director of the Pan-Hellenic Council *MWANAMUGIMU Annual Essay Contest,* unit chairperson of the League of Women Voters, delegate for the Convention of Community Churches, Basileus of Phi Sigma Chapter of Sigma Gamma Rho Sorority, and founder of its Debutante Scholarship Program. She was also an active member of the National Council of Negro Women, The Alpha Wives and the Rosebuds, the friendship group of teachers of Garnet Patterson, as well as the secretary for the Dunbar High School 1933 Alumni Class.

As an active member of People's Community Church for over 40 years, she served as a deaconess, vacation Bible school director, and Sunday school superintendent from 1958 to 1994. Her children and grandchildren participated on a regular basis in church activities and helped her with both Sunday school and vacation Bible school.

The world was her passion, and she traveled extensively, visiting most of the USA and the Caribbean, Western Europe, and Africa. Her many interests included literature, music, and theater. She touched and enriched the lives of all she met.

In Earle Francis Jones's (Little Earle) case, he had generations of family on both his paternal and maternal side that definitely shaped where he was going in life and helped mold the person he is today. Their strong and consistent commitment to education, acquisition of knowledge, community service, honor to country, motivation and confidence to spread your wings to soar, faith in God, courage to face adversity and move through it, being your brother's keeper, etc., has (using a basketball analogy) "cleared the lane" for those who followed.

Earle followed his family legacy well—a legacy set by the courageous family men and women before him, especially his mother and father.

FAMILY

Family is not an important thing. It's *everything*—Michael J. Fox

There are many reasons why family always comes first for Earle. Clearly, his family legacy showed him how it works to your advantage. It has always provided him the support, the love, and the honesty he's come to rely upon. They are the individuals who have known and been with him from the moment he was brought into this world. Whether it was a family vacation with his parents and his sister in the sixties to the New England coast, or spending some time with his grandkids at Cape May, N.J., or the many vacations spent with his sister, niece, and her family in France, at the end of the day, Earle knew he had spent his time surrounded by the people who love him. Some say that when one has his or her family and health, that's all that an individual really needs. Earle believes the reasons why family always comes first are unlimited and endless! He often tells me he came to realize later in life that much of his success has come because he had a supportive family.

Some basic principles Earle and I live by as we both give and receive as family members:

- Family will give you the love you need without you having to grab it out of them—unconditional love

- Your family will always tell you the truth, whether or not you want the honest truth. One may have gotten the typical, "Take that outfit off right now," and the "You were 100 percent wrong." Even if the truth was not sought, you got it, and for that, be thankful and grateful—honesty

- Think of the worst situation and the best situation, and then think of the people who would really be there next to you. Your family, for both—through thick and thin

- Family relationships teach you a set of morals and principles that you take with you to use to survive in the real world—ethical and spiritual guidance

It becomes our responsibility to develop a strong family bond. Lately, many of us have become so wrapped up in technology we forget that real human interactions can be at risk to that development. When out for dinner or spending quality time with the family, put away those electronic devices and actually listen to what your family has to say. If you don't live as close as you would like to with your family, all you have to do is pick up the phone to hear about a family member's day or to gossip. This can help you develop or improve your relationship with your family. Even if you have an amazing family relationship, create, refine, and retell positive, joyful family stories that remind you of the reasons that your family comes first. Earle continues to put family first and lives that example, especially for the younger members of his family.

FAMILY ESSAYS

- **Mr. Dennis Ballard**, Retired Metro Official

- **Dr. Pamela Ballard**, Attending Physician, MedStar National Rehabilitation Hospital

- **Mr. Arthur Carroll**, Retired

- **Ms. Iris Cooper**, Retired Schoolteacher

- **Ms. Portia Deal**, M.A., English Teacher and Special Educator, Prince George County

- **Mrs. Yvonne Delevoye**, Ph.D., Cognitive Psychology, University of Lille, France

- **Mr. Laurent Delevoye**, Ph.D., Physics, University of Lille, France

- **Paul, Alexandre, and Samuel Delevoye**, Students

- **Mrs. Heather Eatmon**, Elementary Schoolteacher

- **Steve Eatmon**, M. Div., Pastor and Youth Director

- **Mr. Curtis Anthony Freeman**, County Commissioner

- **Reverend Jennifer Gatling-Sharpe**, Retired Executive Assistant

- **Mr. Phillip Grasty**, Airline Pilot

- **Ms. Bertha Henson**, Regina & Micaela Burch

- **Mrs. Viola Holloman**, Retired

- **Miss Brittany Jones**, Student, Bowie State University

- **Dr. James Mitchell**, President, Wallace Community College Selma

- **Mrs. Corelette Smith**, Retired High School teacher

- **Mrs. Hazel Taylor**, Retired

- **Ms. Sylvia Turrell**, Ph.D., Retired Professor Emeritus, University of Lille, France

- **Mrs. Terri Watts**, Retired Veteran, Retired Teacher and Author

- **Mrs. Jewell Wiggins**, City of Raleigh-Public Utilities Department

OUR PARENTS LOOKING DOWN
By Sylvia Jones Turrell

The relationship between a child and his parents is very variable and forever changing. At first, the parents look upon this bundle of joy as a fragile sort of subentity of themselves, totally dependent upon them for survival and for growth. The baby, at the same time, recognizes the adults as those who hold the secret to survival, to comfort, and to love. Gradually, the infant attempts to emulate these beings, being rewarded by *ahs* and food, hugs and kisses.

Time brings advances, successes, and failures, and eventually influences from outside the family circle. All the while, the parents watch, prod, lead, push—to ensure the passage of their little one along the road of success as they have envisioned it. The paths actually chosen are not always common agreement! But overall, both the parents and the child aim for success and happiness, with the child wanting also to be the source of happiness, pride, and satisfaction of his parents.

Some people choose to follow the path open and straight before them, for better or for worse. Not Earle: he forged his road; one paved a section at a time; sometimes retreating to readjust his aim. All the time our parents watched. At first with reserve: "He can do more than that" and then, "Not bad, but he's capable of doing better." All the time, Earle said little, but heard and silently heeded our parents because he was keenly aware of the legacy that had been established by those who had gone on before—Sam Jones, Mable Carroll, and so on.

When he decided to take a 90° turn in his path and via Berkeley School of Law, our parents held their breaths for a while. They felt immensely proud of Earle, but also had a huge dose of apprehension—would he, could he make it? Earle's successes at Berkeley, his impact in the organizations, his upward trending career, all these things brought immense joy, pride, satisfaction, and happiness to our parents. But there was just one tinge: Earle was always so far away on the West Coast and them on the East Coast, and his visits back home seemed so short. What about his feelings for family? Did they really know him?

In reality, it was their doubts and fears that were unfounded. As has always been true throughout his life, Earle was building from the inside, and family and its legacy were at the foundation of that structure.

Fate brought Earle back to the DC area just at a time when our parents began to need help. Here was the time for the child to reverse the roles. Indeed, Earle was there to protect our parents, to lead them along their last roads—proving that not only was he a successful person but also a son with unlimited love and devotion.

Earle's attention then began to fix on deeper questions of "family." As the oldest male heir of the Jones-Carroll clan, he felt the responsibility of pursuing the roots and in safe-guarding the heritage and the unity of this family stretched across the expanse of the "Great Pond." Over the past 15 or 20 years, using the modern tools of airplanes, e-mail, Skype, and Web, Earle has forged the lines to tie our family together. The regular Skype connections make it so that children and adults on both sides of the Atlantic keep visual and oral contact. Uncle Earle is a hero to the boys on the French side . . . to such an extent that this year, the 13-year-old nephew was overjoyed to spend 2 weeks with his uncle—a proof of how comfortable they are together and how close the bonds are.

What would our parents have wanted to say to Earle today?

--They are proud of Earle, of the person he has become professionally, an inspiring, handsome, and imposing man. Proud he has achieved the success they knew he could in a world that is so very different from theirs.

--They are proud also of other aspects of him. Mama would cite how happy she is in what he does at church and other community activities. Dad would be ever so happy about Earle's work on the family history and what he does to hold the family together. And both of them would talk about their pride in the role model he has become.

How many times have Earle and I said that we feel that Mom and Dad are really happy—happy with this genuinely united and happy family we have. Mom and Dad are much more than satisfied with what their son has become. Earle is, indeed, the man they envisioned.

The Little Brother That Is More Than "Little"

Since Earle is my "little" brother, he probably never guessed how much I watched and learned from him over the years.

With 4 years between us, for a long time, he was really the little one, following and trusting me (poor thing): jumping up and down in his crib (egged on by me and a cousin) until the slats fell out (my mother was smart enough to know who was at fault); sharing the bunk bed built entirely by Dad. Earle got to be on top and thus, the one to fall out (he didn't even wake up!); partaking in pillow fights with the upstairs neighbor boys (until one hit his head on the bedpost and had to go to the hospital for stitches). Then, our running after the ice-cream truck ("one Popsicle, please"); our watching TV favorites together (Mickey Mouse Club, Howdy Doody, Hopalong Cassidy); our time at Grandmama's (Earle was her "banana boy" and loved her peanut butter, jelly, and butter sandwiches!).

And the little one grew and became more independent. Earle was the neighborhood leader of the bicycle gang, riding miles into the fields (sometimes allowing me to join). As his very beautiful young soprano voice transitioned to a deeper one, he replaced singing with his beloved flute, which he played marvelously—He even had the courage to play a solo at the sixth-grade graduation ceremony (in the photo album, I wrote under his photo "like a bird"). Courage was also at the Boy Scout Fair, where he crossed the entire stadium on a rope bridge 50 or so yards above our heads (as several hundreds of people held their collective breaths). Courage was also listening to rock and roll ("forbidden" in our family) on the radio in his room, despite my dad's threats!

Dependable? Starting from his junior high school days, he maintained his teaching and assistance with Sunday school—which often meant serious schedule juggling! But everyone knew that Earle could be counted on—be it helping my mom with yet another volunteer project or be it his continuous help as a lifesaver with the Kennedy swimming program in Virginia for underprivileged children.

And then the day when he was able to lead me: my swimming class lifesavers test with the endless laps of the crawl. I can remember being so tired that I just wanted to give up. But Earle kept walking on the side of the pool next to me and yelling at me to continue until my second wind came. I didn't even know what a "second wind" was. But the miracle—it came! And thanks to him, I got my diploma!

By this time, our age difference made it that our lives were often separate. But his concerts with the high school orchestras and bands became more numerous and imposing. And as BASKETBALL became a passion of his life, I helped to collect and transfer to the washing machine the contents of his gym bag (which stunk so much that it was not allowed in the house). Gifted for so many things, he was—but never bragging.

The proudest moment? When you're living a childhood together, it's hard to put everything into focus. But certainly, when he said, in all modesty, that he was quitting his job and going back to school—to law school in Berkeley!!—there was blind admiration on my part!! Like a cherry on top of all of those years of shared trust, dependability, and love.

I'm proud that Earle is my brother—he is the best brother a girl could have!! If I try to choose adjectives to describe him, certain ones pop into my head immediately: loving, dependable, trusting, courageous, gifted, modest, leader—everything one wants in a perfect brother.

Sylvia Jones Turrell (Sister)

THE BEST ROLE MODEL

It was New Year's Eve 1995, the middle of my freshman year of high school. I was at home, and the doorbell rang. There stood a man who was asking to see my mom and introduced himself to me as Earle Jones. My mother had been in a few relationships after her divorce, but something about him seemed to be different.

He offered to play basketball with me and get to know me better. We were able to bond over watching football and analyzing what was happening during the game. He wasn't just interested in the relationship with my mother, but with me as well. As my high school years progressed and he and my mom married, he became more and more of the father figure that I needed in my life at the time. He helped with schoolwork and was regularly in attendance at all the important events related to my extracurricular activities: football games, drum line competitions, and band concerts.

He played an important role in my decision to go to college. I applied to nine schools and got accepted to eight of them—University of Florida, Florida State, University of North Carolina Chapel Hill, Duke, North Carolina State, Virginia Commonwealth, University of Georgia, Northwestern, and Florida A&M. We took four separate trips to visit seven of those schools, three of them flights to Chicago, Gainesville, and Tallahassee, one of them a drive to the Raleigh-Durham area to visit the North Carolina schools. His wisdom and insight were outstanding and very instrumental in helping me decide on the school that was the best for me and the direction I wanted to go—which became Florida State University.

I got the opportunity to work with him as an intern while he ran District Cablevision, now Comcast, when I was in high school. I got to see someone with a strong work ethic, dedication to detail, and a tireless problem solver. His insight in moving me toward a major in communications has helped me in the work world. Most jobs are earned with technical skills, but it is actually the "soft" communication skills that allow one to keep and excel on the job. He always gives great insight into things that are not seen and not said in the workplace—things that one must understand in order to survive.

But most of all, the biggest impact he had on me was his mentorship as a role model. For a young black man, that is important, as many of the images throughout the media, in schools, and around in various social networks perpetuated a negative stereotype of how a black man was supposed to act, talk, dress, and conduct himself. He has worked tirelessly to challenge me to buck that trend and not fall into that stereotype—a stereotype that is perpetuated not only by the society at large, but also by many within the black community. We had a long conversation about this on the trip to North Carolina to visit the three colleges I had applied to in the Raleigh-Durham area. Many black youths strive toward a standard of behavior and conduct that is detrimental to their development, and it goes so much deeper than how one wears their pants or the kind of music they listen to. The underlying philosophy and worldview, fed to young black men, by other black people themselves, as well as the media, prevents them from succeeding in various aspects of life— spiritually, academically, socioeconomically, financially, and relationally. He challenged me to rise above many of these messages and philosophies that are perpetuated within the society and raised my awareness to many other messages that are more discreet in nature.

Throughout my college years and into my professional career, he has always had a pervading influence on everything that I do, being very supportive in every way. From college, to seminary, to my time in the business and corporate world, to ministry, he has always been there, and now, as a married man with two kids of my own, I see him as the wise and caring grandfather, willing to do whatever is necessary, willing to support in any way and be there for his grandchildren. I respect Earle Jones greatly for the kind of man he is as I always look up to him because he's much more than a stepfather.

Love You,
Steve (Stepson)

FAITHFUL FATHER AND DEVOTED GRANDFATHER

My father-in-law, Earle, is a wise and caring man who is a blessing to everyone he meets. He is an incredible grandfather to his grandkids, Ryan and Rachael. There is nothing he wouldn't do for them. We are so blessed to have him in our lives.

As long as I have known Earle, he has always been a very kind and welcoming man. When I met his son, Steve, he quickly welcomed me into the family. I have always had the privilege of learning a wise perspective on current events, politics, and history from him. He has a wealth of knowledge that we have learned much from. Whenever Steve or I need advice on a decision that needs to be made, he is always ready to lend a listening ear and share his wisdom and counsel.

I have always been impressed with his diligence in his profession and his service to the community. When he isn't hard at work downtown, he is always helping people—volunteering for a youth club, serving in his church, and in more recent years, spending time with his grandkids.

When my children, Ryan and Rachael, his grandchildren, were born, I had the privilege of witnessing great dedication like no other. From the day they were born, Earle made himself available. Along with Grammy, he helped with early-morning feedings and was always available to hold them and care for them as newborns. From fun sleepovers at the grandparents, to trips to the hospital after injuries, to school Christmas programs, visits to the zoo, cheerleader at soccer games, learning how to swim, playing in the park, his grandchildren can count on him to be there. No distance is too great, and no event is too insignificant. They can count on Granddad!

He is an attentive listener to his oldest grandchild, Ryan, who often has quite a lot to share. Earle will gently share with him his wisdom and encouragement. Rachael, his youngest grandchild, can be a little high-strung at times, but his patience with her is quite remarkable. When she was a newborn and still trying to make sense of the world, he would carry her on his strong shoulders, walking around the house, giving her a different view of her surroundings, and calming her down. His peaceful presence was the calm she needed.

We have enjoyed numerous adventures with Granddad. In the summer, we have enjoyed fun trips to the beach with Granddad and Grammy. Recently, he took Ryan on a train ride adventure. It is a memory Ryan will never forget. They rode into Baltimore and shared their love for trains as they watched the trains pass by en route and at the station. They are sure to have many more adventures together!

When times have been tough, you would never know it, because Granddad has made sure his grandkids can live like a prince and princess! They have been so blessed by his care and generosity. Earle is a wonderful grandfather, father, father-in-law and husband, leaving a wonderful legacy for all of us.

Heather Eatmon (Daughter-in-law)

MY OLDER BROTHER/BRO-N-LAW

While most of us don't spend a lot of time with our sister's husband or even can say that you admire him for more than he married my sister, Earle came to be a big brother in many ways. His demeanor is sometimes stern, but understanding; he fiercely protects his own. Yep, I even mean his in-laws. And he even takes their advice!

I had the pleasure of living with my sister, Linda, and Earle for a number of years, when I first moved to Northern Virginia from Maryland. I remember evenings while we were preparing dinner, Earle would bring us up-to-date with the news of the day, and we were his audience. I learned so much from his "updates"— not only in what he was sharing but the manner in which he shared. Never condescending or preachy, just a genuine way of passing on information he thought one would be interested in.

Earle had complained about his foot on several occasions. I had heard a friend at work rave about her podiatrist being the greatest thing since the beginning of time! She talked about how he had given her a complete foot examination, clipped her toenails, and gave her a foot message, so I went to the doctor thinking he would do the same for me, and when I got there, I was asked if I was a diabetic. I answered no. The PA told me that they could only examine my feet for problems, and if no problems existed, then no massage or clipping of toenails. Needless to say, I was quite disappointed. But when I asked to speak with the podiatrist, he explained everything to me. So when I left, I really was satisfied. Well, weeks later, when Earle mentioned the problem with the pain in his feet, I told him about the podiatrist. Now, I never bothered to check with Earle about the outcome of his visit. But just now in 2016, I found out that he went to that podiatrist, and he solved Earle's foot problems and even clipped his toenails and gave him a foot message!

Once, after I had gotten my credit scores all corrected and was finally in the position to purchase a car, Earle was walking past me in the garage and said, "Jeni, don't allow anyone to influence you to purchase something you really don't want." Well, now, I wondered why he made that statement to me out of the blue! I started trying to rationalize that thought. I had not long started dating my "now" husband, and Earle really didn't know a lot about him. So here Earle was thinking that Charles was influencing me to purchase a car that I really didn't want! While all along, Charles was trying to reason with me to purchase a more sensible vehicle.

One evening, about 6 p.m., I had come home from work and was going down the back steps to check on some plants we had down in the ponderosa. As I approached the bottom step, I saw what I thought was a large snake. So, of course, I started screaming. At that moment, no one was home, but soon after, I heard a garage door go up and heard Earle calling out our names, as he always did when he came in and cars were in the garage. Earle continued to call my name as he went through the house. Eventually, he heard me yelling outside downstairs, "Earle, Earle, there's a snake! Kill it, kill it!" I'm terrified of snakes! Which he knows!! Here come Earle rushing down the steps, all suited down, briefcase in hand, ready to do battle. He drops the briefcase, grabs the shovel, which stands nearby, and pounds the snake to smithereens.

Now those incidents, as well as many others, told me a lot about my "brother"-in-law. He's willing to listen, willing to take your suggestions/advice, and fiercely protective of his family.

When you get to know Earle, you'll find out soon enough that he can hold a conversation with everyone and even seek out advice from the best or the least of us. He takes pride in his family as well as his friends' advancements. He means a lot to the family, and his advice is always warranted. He has come to be the older brother now in the family. And if you need a snake killed, call him. He'll blast it for you. J

Reverend Jennifer H. Gatling-Sharpe (Sister-in-law)

THE RIGHT MAN FOR MY NEPHEW

When my sister remarried, her son, Steve, was a teen. Earle Jones entered into our lives, and more importantly, he became my nephew's stepfather. Now, I'll say up front, I have a real soft spot in my heart for my nephew, so I was looking very carefully as to how the remarriage would impact him. I was looking for certain characteristics, whether I had a right to or not. He had to be steadfast, supportive, and loyal. It was a given, he had to live a Christian life.

From the very start, I could see that Earle had all these characteristics and much more, but I wanted to see consistency in his actions toward Steve.

Steadfast—Earle took the time to see what Steve needed in a father role. As a result, he shaped his approach and actions to developing a relationship with Steve that was not a threat or in competition with the mother-son relationship. He carved out areas that he could add value to Steve's interests: sports, music, world news, religion, history, etc. They had a terrific time traveling to about six or seven colleges in Steve's junior year in high school, which made it easier for Steve to select a college. Also, I think they were able to catch a few professional basketball and football games along the way. Earle was there for Steve, and trust was earned.

Supportive—When Steve was trying to decide which college to attend, Earle sought out people Steve could talk to in order to help in the process and provided information that helped the process. In fact, it was Earle knowing a person at FAMU that recommended a Florida State visit—which was not on Steve's list at all. They went to Florida State, and the rest is history—Steve graduated from FSU 4 years later.

Loyalty—The type of loyalty a teen needs is unconditional love, regardless of the situation and the "sharing" pains a teen can experience in a new marriage. Earle was loyal to Steve in action and deed—Earle was consistent, reliable and faithful—he walked his talk with Steve. Plus, Earle treated my sister with great respect and love.

Earle passed my test. To this day, he probably never knew he had a test; however, being a high school teacher, it was only natural that I look at it this way. Earle has modeled the type of father and husband that Steve can now use in his own family.

........Now For My Big Sister
As I visited my sister and family I began to talk to Earle about his travels. We shared the same interest in history. I have such a passion for learning about the past. If I had to attend college again, I would take African American Studies. I have learned so much from him. We would sit around the house, and he would tell me about his travels to Africa and other places. I am so amazed at his wealth of knowledge. The stories he told were so exciting. I will always remember the stories and his beautiful paintings from across the world. He even purchase some from little old Ahoskie, N.C. I think about Earle and his relationship with Linda and Steve, and I realize he was what they needed in order to fulfill their family unit. He is a warm and loving man who seeks the best for my sister and nephew. He shares some of the best qualities of our father, whom I love dearly and respect.
Corelette (Cocoa) Smith (Sister-in-law)

THE "GREATEST" GREAT-UNCLE

Even though we are young (Paul, 13, Alex, 12, and Sam, 10), we have a lot of great memories with the "greatest" great-uncle ever—we just call him Uncle Earle. He has visited us in France many times, and we have visited him in Virginia many times. We always find Uncle Earle:

- Always smiling

- Never bored with us or us with him

- Wanting to do the things that please us

- Looking after us to make sure we are OK

- Liking what we prefer—SPORTS!!!—basketball and American football

He plays basketball with us outside and has showed us many moves to help us in our own game. When we see Uncle Earle playing and driving to the basket, we think of Shaq because he is so much bigger and taller than we are.

If we have a question about family history, we go to him because he knows everything. He really knows our family history and works hard to keep it for us. He cares about us always knowing our family history so much that he asked Paul to start to learn what he has done over the years on Ancestry.com. This way, Uncle Earle can pass it on to Paul to be the keeper of the family history when he gets old.

Uncle Earle cares about everyone in the family and his friends too. He treats everyone really nice and with respect. We are proud to call him Uncle Earle.

Oops, we almost forgot—he makes us say grace before we eat—Every time!!!

Paul, Alex, and Sam Delevoye (Great-nephews)

THE SON-IN-LAW FATHER'S VISIT

By having Earle as a son-in-law for almost 20 years almost gives me too many things to talk about. But one thing I fondly remember is when he brought his father to Ahoskie, N.C., to visit us in 2003. Mr. Jones was 88 years old.

Mr. Jones always liked to visit different places and was looking forward to visiting our small town. Earle and Linda brought him down to spend a weekend with my husband and myself. He said the Hertford County area reminded him of the time his family lived in a small town in Newtonville, New Jersey, back in the 1930s. He loved talking about farming and the crops that grew in our area for market: cotton, tobacco, peanuts, soy beans, watermelons, and cucumbers.

Earle was trying to anticipate and respond to his father's every need so he would not be a "burden" on us. Well, at 88, Mr. Jones was as spry as someone half his age. Finally, Earle and Linda left to visit other relatives, and they were spending the night with my other daughter while Mr. Jones spent 2 nights with us. We were glad they were gone so we were free to really enjoy his company. We even invited our neighbor over to meet him because Mr. Jones was such an interesting person and had so many stories to share with us and us with him.

When I was talking to Mr. Jones, I saw the care, concern, and strength of commitment expressed in how he took care of his family and extended family through some really tough times and how he went back to college to get advanced degrees to ensure he could send his kids to college. Through his volunteer work that he did in the community to uplift the plight of blacks and his participation in the 1963 March on Washington, as well as the 1995 Million Man March at the age of 80—I just kept seeing my son-in-law Earle in him.

He was so respectful of our home and showed such gratitude of the simple meals we prepared for him—truly a humble man. No one would have known the accomplishments he had achieved in his lifetime—one of the first black scientists to work for the Bureau of Standards, naval officer, elected into one of the prestigious science societies for auditory and sound in the 1950s, advanced degrees when most blacks could barely graduate from high school, and so on. He sounded so much like his son and my son-in-law, Earle. I wondered if he saw the similarities.

Mr. Jones would be so proud today to see Earle is a "chip off the old block"—like they say, "the apple didn't fall far from the tree." I could clearly see how my son-in-law Earle got to be the man he is because of the man his father was.

All I can say is Earle's a great man in his own right and a wonderful son-in-law—he's always been there for me and my family.

Mrs. Viola Holloman (Vi) (mother-in-law)

A COOL, CARING GUY

"Be completely humble and gentle; be patient, bearing with one another in love. Make every effort to keep the unity of the Spirit through the bond of peace."—Ephesians 4:2–3

One of the things I admire so much in Earle is his support for his wife and her support for him. It is a beautiful thing to see a husband and wife totally supportive of each other. Linda started the Christmas party custom before she met and married Earle. When they married, he supported her and made it an annual custom that is now known in both families.

Likewise, when Earle's father became ill with dementia, Linda teamed with Earle to provide the best support they could find. She worked with Earle to ensure his father had all of his needs met. One incident comes to mind that I even chuckle at today. As his father's dementia was getting worse, some people were trying to take advantage of a senior living alone by trying to befriend him just to get inside the house to steal things. One occasion, Earle noticed his father's TV was missing and the lock on the basement window had been broken. His father couldn't recall what happened. After notifying the police, Earle and Linda were determined to find out who was entering into the house and taking things while his father was sleeping. They donned dark clothing, hoods, and caps, and waited outside the house by the bushes to see if they could catch the person taking advantage of his father. I started to call Earle and Linda, "Batman and Robinette." Earle supports Linda and his marriage, and she does as well.

I knew both of Earle's parents for many years prior to their deaths. His mother was my first cousin. I see today many of the values, characteristics, and traits that both his mother and father set the example for when they raised him. Earle's mother was one of the most generous persons I knew. She paid for me to take a trip with her to Germany to see the Oberammergau Passion Play. She was extremely refined in the arts and well traveled and willing to share her knowledge with all. Any task she took on, she gave it her all. She was very community focused, supported her alumni sorority in providing public service to the underserved in DC, her faith was well-known, she was a Sunday school superintendent and taught Sunday school for many years. She was very family oriented.

On the other hand, his father worked to break barriers and create opportunities in the communities for young African Americans to expose them to the arts. He created the black maxi circus and developed a community program, caroling for dollars that raised several thousands of dollars for the underserved each Christmas. In addition, they each valued education and attained multiple degrees themselves.

Sound familiar? Earle had a foundation and role models from his parents that helped to create the man he is today. Now, you can lead a horse to water, but you cannot make him drink. So the caring, giving, concerned for others, devoted husband, father, grandfather, respectful, and overall intelligent man he became is because of what he did with what he was given.

Cousin Hazel Taylor

WHO IS UNCLE EARLE?

That is a good question. And through the years, every second I have had with him would help me learn more and discover an incredible family leader. Cultured, powerful, caring . . . Even though for most of my life, Uncle Earle and I lived on opposite sides of the Atlantic Ocean—me in France and him in the U.S., these are some of the special moments that come to my mind.

(Five years old in Montréal, Canada) Going to the baseball stadium with my uncle and getting a hot dog . .. Came back with a hard baseball cap that I might have worn to bed!

(Seven years old in Washington, DC) Waiting for the taxi to take us downtown on the front porch at my grandparents' house on a warm and humid summer evening. My uncle would rush up to me and share a big hug with a spin—that is how my uncle always greeted me after a year (or more) of not seeing each other. The Washington days were great because we would have quality time together: bicycling around the corner, down the sidewalks of Somerset Place; hours of throwing a baseball in the garden; but most of all, I remember learning so much during our outings to the Washington zoo to see all those animals that Uncle Earle knew all about.

(Twelve years old in Denver) Welcoming us to his home, when we visited Denver. Yet another visit to the zoo, but this time, to ride an elephant!

But more important than the ride was my change in perspective. Indeed, during that summer, it was the first time that I saw his "secret" life. I realized for the first time how important my uncle was: all those pictures of him with important people; advanced degrees, awards, and certificates! I would watch him read, listen to the radio, and watch TV—any media to learn more, to keep up with the changing world. Maybe the most striking yet was to discover his interest in the Egyptian culture. Pictures, sculptures, books . . . what a collection! It was amazing, and from that day on, I realized how knowledgeable my uncle was and how much of a leader he was becoming.

And this new insight evolved as I became an adult. Every visit became a new discovery with a friendly relative becoming little by little a father figure. When my grandmother passed away, Uncle Earle became for me the center pillar of the Jones family because, amongst other things, he welcomed me in his home. He opened his immediate family to me, as my grandparents did before. He gave me a place to stay and made me feel like a part of him.

This kindness and warmth gave me the desire, opportunity, and strength to maintain my American roots.

The importance of family became even more remarkable through the years, with the time spent sharing pictures, working on the family tree, taking time to share old generational stories, and even taking time off work to drive up to New Jersey to see extended family. Even if modest and not always outspoken, Uncle Earle's values on behalf of family are immense; they have spread and made it possible for me to pass on the American roots to my own children in France. And for that, I am forever thankful.

Yvonne Delevoye (Niece)

UNCLE EARLE, THE MAN WHO . . .

While many people who have achieved as much as Earle could be inaccessible and distant, it is not the case with our uncle Earle. On the contrary, Earle is a person who always has the reassuring, thoughtful, and rational word. The first time I really met Earle (who is also "Uncle Earle" for our three boys) was during summer 1998 when Yvonne, his niece (and at that time, my future wife), and I went to Washington, DC, and were invited to stay in Linda and Earle's home in Vienna, Virginia.

There is a specific moment I remember from this visit. On the first day of our stay, Linda and Earle took us for a tour of their house, and in his office, a few pictures on the wall impressed me a great deal, showing Earle with some famous people (including a former president and a few famous athletes). This is where I became aware of Earle's achievements in his professional life! One picture really caught my attention: the one showing Earle (6 foot 3!!) side by side with Magic Johnson (6 foot 8!!), the Lakers' legend. I am a basketball fan (more than a former president's fan), and this kind of picture does impress a lot. I remember asking if it was really Magic Johnson, but there was no possible doubt about it.

It turns out that 15 years later, while my three boys (who play basketball and follow the NBA games) were discussing and comparing former and actual NBA players—with detailed stats related to each player, I entered into the conversation to mention that picture of Uncle Earle with Magic Johnson. Obviously, they did not believe me . . . until the next time they visited Aunt Linda and Uncle Earle's house. And they saw for themselves! They were at least as speechless as I was 15 years earlier!!

He is also someone who takes care of others. On several occasions, I have seen him take care and watch over his family, from his dad to his grandkids. I especially appreciate how he has given us, Yvonne and me, love and attention for the last 20 years. For all that, he is a model to me, as I am sure that he will be a model for my children.

And he will be forever the Man Who Met Magic Johnson.

Laurent (Nephew-in-law)

REFLECTIONS OF ADMIRATION AND LOVE

Life's experiences between childhood and adulthood can become vague or distant. In spite of this, the mind can recall and reminisce over the most meaningful memories; the ones that can last for a lifetime and pass from generation to generation.

As I was growing up in Newtonville, New Jersey, and Earle was growing up in Washington, DC, the 148.1 miles between the two areas and infrequent visits did not prevent me from enjoying the times that we shared family fun together and built a family bond of friendship. Although I cherish those childhood moments, the ones that have secured and locked the bond of friendship occurred during my years living within the Washington, DC, metropolitan area.

Precious moments: The precious moments that lock our bond of friendship include: watching your joyfulness and fun-spirited mood when you moved from your home in Silver Spring, Maryland, to Vienna, Virginia; seeing your exuberant temperament during your wedding reception and your continual attentiveness to your guests' needs; watching you patiently try to explain your position to your dad when he was unable to understand your position on a situation (just not getting it); hearing your wisdom disclosed with gentleness and genuine concern when I had to withdraw from a business partnership; following your logic as we discussed a personal relationship decision, and you assuring me that I was "correct" and "sane"; and, of course, listening to my spirit-free and carefree attitude and thoughts when I was going through my rebellious stage after my divorce. Even though you probably do not remember, I remember your facial expression of "OKAY." It seemed as if you were thinking, "Are you going to be all right, cousin?" Your response showed compassion and sensitivity for my circumstances—you could have lectured me; you didn't. This was truly a trying time for me, and you were there for me—THANKS!!!

Never too busy to check: With your busy schedule of family and life, you showed your love during my life-challenging times; my hospital stay; celebrating my master's degree; inquiring about the welfare of my children and grandchildren; defending my health condition when a lady questioned why I was using a cane; and other occasions throughout time—the little and powerful jesters that clinch the bond of friendship. You include my family and me when you have events, whether it is for the holiday, summer picnic, weddings, hanging out (far and few, I must work on improving that ratio), and France family visits. My family and I appreciate the love that you express each time we meet, regardless of the time span between gatherings. Earle, your kindness, compassion, concern, and love for others are far above the natural realm; it is Christ-centered.

God has truly blessed me through you. I admire that you are a humble man who does not look down on others but reaches down to help others up. My prayer is that God will grant you peace, grace, and blessings beyond your earthly realm of comprehension.

Portia Deal (Cousin)

UNCLE EARLE
By Brittany Jones

How can you describe,
an uncle so great.
Who states that their love and support for you,
will never break?

Awesome, intelligent,
and fun to be around
Also you always see a smile on his face,
and never a frown.

Whenever I may come across a struggle,
or my day is not "as bright."
He lifts me up with motivation and advises me,
that everything is going to be all right.

I'm grateful for his unconditional love,
since I was a newborn girl,
I'm truly blessed to have him in my life,
Thank you, Uncle Earle!!!

LIFE-DEFINING SUMMER—FROM CHERRY PICKER TO LAWYER

According to Earle, working on a trash truck and gathering wild cherry leaves for my father-in-law one hot South Jersey summer helped him to decide to continue his education. He still speaks of how life changing this experience was for him.

Earle's father and my mother were brother and sister. The families lived in different states when we were growing up. Uncle Earle would always bring our cousins, "little Sylvia and little Earle," to visit with us for a couple of weeks during the summer. Most of my brothers and sisters were older than Earle, but we all played and worked together. We have fond memories of looking forward to the July Sunday school picnic in Wildwood, New Jersey, when our cousins, Sylvia and Earle, would make our lives more enjoyable with their company. Earle was always a "sweetheart."

After working with my father-in-law that summer, Earle's comments became more about what he was doing to prepare himself for college and beyond. He did not know he would become a lawyer then, but he knew that cherry picking and trash picking would not define his future—education would. He was somewhat reserved, but you could see his determination in how he approached the work he was asked to do by family members. Always very dependable and trustworthy, you could see his concern for others then.

Also, during that summer, I saw what a kind-hearted and caring person he was, who expressed genuine concern for the misfortunes of others and affection for his New Jersey family, even those of us whose behavior could be characterized as beyond eccentric.

We really have come to appreciate all the work he has done on our family tree, helping each of us to understand our legacies. Especially all the data he tirelessly enters in Ancestry.com that helps the younger generation.

When our cousins visit from France, Earle makes sure we see each other. He makes an effort to attend each of my granddaughters' concerts at the National Cathedral School and ensuring that she could attend a summer tennis camp (paying the enrollment fees and helping with transportation to and from tennis sessions).

Earle remains available as a supportive family member for advice, counsel, and just listening.

Bertha Henson, Regina, and Micaela Burch
Your Devoted Cousins

REAL DEAL EARLE

My family lived across the street in Ahoskie, North Carolina, from Linda's family for longer than I can remember; we are cousins. Whenever Linda and Earle would visit her mother, they would naturally walk across the street to visit, especially when we were out in the yard. As a result, I got to know Earle pretty well, and we would have some lively conversations on the subject of the day.

One conversation still stands out in my mind. I was running for the County Board of Commissioners, and Earle was, without lecturing, providing me some advice based on his experiences with politicians over the world. It was quite simple: "Remain honest and true—and put God first," he said.

I thought, *WOW, that's it?* Then, I got what he meant—do not try to dress up your ideas and sell them to your constituents; instead, sell them on the merits of what your ideas will do for them. No smoke and mirrors and magic tricks to win their vote. They will see through it. Not only did it work for me, I passed it on to my adult son and use it quite often in my work as a county commissioner.

The way Earle presents himself puts you at ease because he is at ease with himself. You have a sense that he cares for and is concerned about you. I've always said, "God gave me a third eye to assess people." I've never had a bad vibe about Earle. I've learned how simple things can be if you just walk in truth and honesty.

Even though much of our conversations have been around public policy, Earle's advice and guidance can be used in any area of life. He will give you reasons or examples to validate what he is saying and help you see the practicality in it. I've tried to pattern what I do around what I've seen in him.

Earle is the REAL DEAL—no fluff, just genuine care and concern for his fellow man.

Curtis Anthony Freeman (Cousin by marriage)
Hertford County Board of Commissioners

THE NICEST NEPHEW EVER

Earle is my sister's son, and I've known him since birth. Growing up, you could clearly see the honesty and dependability in him. He was always doing things with my sister at Sunday school to help the kids and the church, even though he was really busy at his school.

He enjoyed music and basketball very much in school. Today, when I visit his home, I see that he still does love the two. He and his son, Steve, watch sports on TV and discuss the players and the game strategy like pros.

Earle was always there for my mother and his grandmother, Mrs. Mable Carroll. Even though during most of his early adult life he lived in Denver, he would come back to visit, and my sister and mother were so proud of him being a lawyer and how he never forgot his roots.

He is a good man, loves his family, and supports his friends. He has a way at seeing the good in people and will help you out of a bad situation. Earle will help you to understand why things are the way they are and not the way you want them to be.

He is the best of my sister and his father. They would be very proud to see the man he is today.

I am fortunate to live in the metro DC area and get to read about him in the paper when he does great things in the cable industry or see him in the society pages of *The Afro* for some event he has supported and attended.

I am always pleased to see how he always honors my sister's life by recognizing her each year in the memorial section of the *Washington Post* on the date of her birthday. He will never forget his mother and father and the lessons they taught him growing up.

He is the nicest person I know.

Uncle Arthur Carroll

THE FAMILY UNIFIER

First of all, let me start off by saying that I'm the youngest child of Isaac and Juanita Grasty. Earle's mother and my mother were cousins. Being the youngest, I was a couple of decades separated from my sisters and Earle.

I was in my late 20s by the time that I had any interactions with Earle. One of the things I credit him for is bringing the widely scattered family members together regularly with the Christmas celebrations that he and his wife, Linda, host.

My immediate family and I have been greatly enriched by the contacts that we make whenever we attend these events. I couldn't thank him enough for the time and effort that he and his family invest in events. I know it's not easy or cheap to host these gatherings, but Earle and Linda make it look easy.

When my mother fell ill, I was in Denver, Colorado, just starting training at United Airlines. One of the first family members that I saw when I made it to the hospital hours later was Earle. I was obviously concerned about my mother's health, but I do recall that he was there with his calm, reassuring demeanor keeping the family bonds strong.

To sum up what Earle has been throughout my life is a uniting energy in the family. I know that I would not be as close to some of my family if it were not for him.

Thank you, Earle!!!
Phillip Grasty (Cousin)

FROM THE MITCHELL-NEWSOME FAMILY MEMBERS
(Cousins by marriage)

I have come to know Earle from the Mitchell-Newsome family reunions we hold every 2 years. I had seen him there with Linda, my cousin, over the years but did not have an opportunity to interact with him. It was not until I chaired the last couple of reunions that I actually spent some time with him. My observation was that Earle is one of the most attentive and kindest persons I've met. He's always there to lend a hand when needed. He doesn't seem to mind doing anything for anyone. He is just the most considerate and kindest person. Earle and Linda are an adorable couple and happy family. I've really enjoyed working with both of them.

Best wishes, Earle!!!

~ Mrs. Jewell Wiggins

When I think of Earle, I see a man who is supportive, admirable, and doused with insurmountable compassion for others! What a man!

Be blessed, my cousin-in-law.

~ Mrs. Terri Watts

Earle is a quiet and effective leader who truly espouses the principle, lead and serve by example. He is, and continues to be, a positive force and source of support for the Mitchell-Newsome family.

~ Dr. James Mitchell, Ph.D.

Linda introduced Earle to Pam and me at one of our first Mitchell-Newsome family reunions. I was immediately impressed by his quiet, easygoing demeanor. At family and social gatherings following that reunion, Earle impressed me as an individual with intellect, compassion for others, and fun loving . . . complemented by his devotion to his wife and family. However, when the music starts, do not get between Earle and the dance floor!

~ Mr. and Mrs. Dennis (Pamela) Ballard

Could this be a relative of the famous actor? His name and striking resemblance raised the question—sadly resolved when Cousin Linda Paige told me no—but Earle shows a commanding dignity in this own right. At our 2015 Mitchell-Newsome Family Reunion, Earle's presence was a complement to the celebration. He was obviously a delighted participant, but more than that, he was a proud encouragement to Linda Paige in her participation—clearly the wind beneath her wings.

~ Ms. Iris Newsome Cooper

FAMILY PHOTOS

Sylvia, 5 & Earle, 18 months

Earle, Mom & Sister

Earle, 3 & Sylvia, 7

Earle Sr. and Brother Arthur—
Family Picnic, ca. 1960s

Summer visit to DC, 1983

Earle Sr. and nephew Marc, 2003

Family Christmas in DC, 1987

Wedding Day—1999

The" In-laws" at Jennifer & Charles Wedding—2006

Cousins Portia and
daughter Missy—2015

Cousins Hazel, Bertha, Regina , Micaela and Uncle Arthur—2014

The boys watching Basketball game—2013

France family visit to Vienna, Va—2013

Aunt Evelyn & Father, Yvonne & Laurent—2001

Earle and Linda with parents—1999

Linda & Sisters Jennifer, Corelette—2004

Earle & Niece Nawel—2011

Earle & Mother—1987

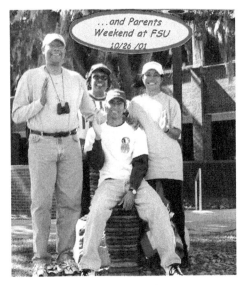

...and Parents Weekend at FSU 10/26/01

Earle, Linda, Steve - Florida State—2001

The Jones Family - Steve & Heather's Wedding—2010

Granddad's
Princess—20 mo.

Steve, Heather, Ryan, Rachael

Granddad's drummer—age 2

Cape May Family Vacation - 2015

Ryan loves Big Trucks - 2013

Miss Rachael - 2 months

Rachael's Birth - 2014

Ryan's Birth - 2012

Doing the "Bump" - 2001

CHURCH

"The church was not merely a thermometer that recorded the ideas and principles of popular opinion; it was a thermostat that transformed the mores of society." Martin Luther King Jr.

Attending church is a visible, tangible expression of our love and worship toward God. It is where we can gather with other believers to publicly bear witness of our faith and trust in God, something that is required of all Christians (Matt. 10:32–33)—and it is where we can bring Him offerings of praise, thanks, and honor, which are pleasing to Him. The psalmist wrote, "I will declare Your name to my brethren; In the midst of the assembly I will praise You" (Psa. 22:22).

As early as Earle can remember, he attended church with his family. Starting from his middle school days, Earle was involved in leadership and volunteer roles at the People's Community Church in northeast Washington DC. His mother was the Sunday school superintendent and taught Sunday school at their church for several decades, and Earle was her able assistant—which often meant serious juggling of his schedule. But everyone knew that Earle could be counted on, whether it was helping his mother with yet another volunteer project or teaching Sunday school.

Rev. David Creech was the senior pastor of People's for over 50 years until his death in 2013, and a great friend of the family. As time permitted over the years, Earle would return for visits to People's. After his mother passed in 1996, it became a symbol of reverence and respect to visit People's in honor of the roles she played at the church. Reverend Creech was at our wedding celebration, and when Earle's sister visited from France with her young children in the '70s and '80s, they would also visit People's. It is true that going to church doesn't make you a Christian any more than going to a garage makes one an automobile. However, acts and expressions of Christian values are a testimony to the heart of a Christian who has accepted Christ. Earle always walked his Christian values—in a quiet, unassuming way.

In the mid-'90s, Earle moved back to the DC area to care for his very ill mother and aging father. His mother passed soon after his return, and his father developed Alzheimer's. During this difficult time, Earle became a member of Antioch Baptist Church in Fairfax, Virginia, in 1997. The church, its focus, mission, leadership, and members have been a stable refuge for Earle.

Sometimes church and community can be seen as the flip side of the same coin—the acts and beliefs of the believers can be the means to transform the customs of society and provide economic and social benefits. Several researchers have identified the social benefits that churches bring to

Worship Center

Ministry Center

communities, including: providing help to poor and vulnerable individuals in the community, improving marriage relationships, decreasing violence among one another, increasing moral community obligations, and promoting charitable contributions and volunteering. Being a member of a religious community can increase one's duty to serve others in the community. Churches help communities complete vitally important social projects, for which the government would need to fund if churches did not provide such support.

Earle's mother and grandmother were key influences to his early start in church and faithful attendance that continues today. His father impressed on him the social benefits' side that church can bring to communities through volunteer service for individuals in the community or the nation in general. Many of Earle's youth volunteer projects in church were community focused—serving as a lifeguard with the Kennedy family swimming program in Virginia for underprivileged children. The same focus continued throughout college, law school, and his professional career.

At his current church, Earle served as a commitment counselor for many years, on the Career Development ministry, and currently serves faithfully on the parking ministry. Find yourself a good church and *let your "works" speak for you!!!*

CHURCH FAMILY ESSAYS

- **Mrs. Mary Alexander**, Retired Educator

- **Rev. Dr. Marshall L. Ausberry Sr.**, Senior Pastor, Antioch Baptist Church

- **Mr. Arthur Coles**, Antioch Parking Ministry

- **Mr. Samuel Harris**, Antioch Parking Ministry

- **Mr. Larry Hester**, Retired Military and Business Executive

- **Mrs. Carrie Hester,** Retired Educator

- **Mr. Richard "Spike" Jones**, Retired Program Director, Army Audit Agency
  Certified Fraud Examiner and Tax Professional

- **Mrs. Linda Stephen-Jones**, Retired Air Force Family Program Director and
  Certified Christian Life Coach

- **Rev. Melvin Jones**, Executive Pastor, Antioch Baptist Church

- **Ms. Keitha Johnson**, Director of Ministry Services & Media, Antioch Baptist Church

- **Mr. Leroy C. Latten**

- **Mr. Allen Sample**

- **Rev. Bernard Snowden Jr.**, Pastor of Family Life, Antioch Baptist Church

- **Mrs. Abigail Taylor**, Retired Educator

- **Mr. Curtis Taylor**, Col., U.S. Army (Ret.) Director, Information Systems Group, Advanced Systems
  Development Inc.

A HUMBLE MAN

As I reflect on Earle Jones, several observations come to mind.

First, my observation of Earle is that he is a man who desires deeply to live a life that is pleasing to God.

I have seen evidence of this in his interaction with his family. Earle displays a deep love and commitment to his lovely wife, Linda. Truly, he models his marriage role according to Ephesians 5:25 (ESV): "Husbands, love your wives, as Christ loved the church and gave himself up for her . . ." Truly, Earle has shown a deep commitment to his wife over the years of their marriage. During Linda's health challenge, Earle was constantly by her side, serving her and comforting her along the way. Another example of Earle's devotion to family was evident when Stephen was in high school and was wrestling with the pressures of being a popular student and the temptations that go along with being a teenager. Earle and Linda worked as a team and brought Stephen to the church. They trusted the church to interact with him.

Because of their working as a team, Stephen made some tremendous growth in his personal walk with the Lord at a pivotal time in his life. The results of their efforts are seen in that Stephen is a wonderful Christian man, husband, and father today.

Second, Earle is a very successful businessman. In an age where there is a tremendous amount of self-promotion, Earle is one of the humblest men that I know. As a successful business executive, he could very easily shine the star on himself. Instead, he humbles himself and serves. At Antioch, this successful business executive humbles himself and serves in the parking ministry. I remember some cold Sunday mornings when I drove into the parking lot. Earle is there with a hat, coat, and gloves on, trying to keep warm, all the while greeting members and guests with a warm and friendly smile as they arrive.

Third, Earle is highly thought of in our local church community. He has an excellent reputation. He also has been involved in mentoring others. He is not one who rests on his accomplishments of the past. Again, Earle is a man who wants to live a life that is pleasing to God!

Finally, I thank God for Earle, not only for the few items mentioned above, but for me personally. Earle is a person who has encouraged me so many times, and probably is unaware of doing so. When I see a man who is as accomplished as he is, who takes the time to encourage others, including the preacher, that is a real blessing! It is a pleasure and joy to serve as Earle's pastor.

God bless you, Brother Earle! Keep up the good work!

Pastor Marshal L. Ausberry Sr.
Sr. Pastor, Antioch Baptist Church
Fairfax Station, Virginia

HUMILITY, JOY, SINCERITY, AND FAITH

No matter the weather or circumstance, I can see Earle's humility, joy, sincerity, and faith. It's not one experience or situation that I reflect upon. When I see him serving with the parking ministry or entering or leaving worship, he is genuine. Earle walks, serves, and lives with humility and joy. No matter the weather outside or what may be going on in his personal life, I can see the joy of the Lord in his expression and countenance. I cherish our discussions, no matter the length, because when Earle asks how I'm doing or asks how's the family, I know his words are genuine. And when I ask how his wife, Sister Linda, is doing, his eyes light up with excitement. I can see the love he has for her, his concern for her health . . . his eyes and expression. Earle is a committed Christian man whom I deeply admire.

Brother Earle, you are an awesome Christian man whom God has truly blessed. May God continue to bless you.

Rev. Melvin E. Jones
Executive Pastor, Antioch Baptist Church

"STEADY"—defined as: to be firmly fixed, supported, balanced, not shaking, and not moving.

All of us have heard of "Steady Eddie." Don't know the man. Never met the man. But I do know Steady Earle, Earle Jones, whom I met in 1997 and have observed his Christian walk and talk for many years.

Steady Earle, one who I know to be a loving husband to his wife, Linda, and a model father to his son, Steve. One who has been devoted to his family and one who has been faithful and committed in his service to his church, Antioch Baptist Church. Steady Earle, one who can be described biblically by the synonyms of "steady": steadfast, immovable, fixed, continuous, and safe. 1 Corinthians 15:58, "Therefore my brethren, be ye steadfast, unmovable, always abounding in the work of the Lord," Hebrew 12:2, "Let us keep our eyes fixed on Jesus." Psalm 34:1, "I will bless the Lord at all times, His praise shall continually be in my mouth." Psalm 91:2, "I will say unto the Lord, He is my refuge and my fortress: my God; in Him will I trust." That is Earle Jones—Steady Earle—my friend, who I always want in my corner. A GEM!!!

Deacon Larry and Carrie Hester, Antioch Baptist Church

"THINKER"

The world places a premium on what is considered to be great minds. Persons like Cornell West and Michael Eric Dyson reflect this as "African American Intellectuals." I have found that Mr. Earle Jones is every bit a "Thinker" and qualified through his academic training and professional career to speak to issues in the community but upholds the biblical standard.

I first met Earle when I went to his home for a Christmas fellowship, the Young Adult Ministry (YAM's) hosted by his wife, Linda, who was the director for the ministry back in 2002. We just had casual conversation. I knew a little of his political involvement, little of him being an executive in the corporate world. Later, a men's conference in 2007 with Herb Lusk speaking, we began to talk more about issues in the community. Later, that would be followed by e-mails or articles regarding social, economic, and political issues. He shared with me the importance of a citizen being involved and keeping abreast in local government, more so than state and national levels. We have more control over who we put in office in local politics. When I see Earle, I "brake" for him. If it is in the parking lot when I arrive at church on Sunday morning, I stop and wind down my car window (as long as no one is behind me). I see him sometimes in the food room when the men from the parking ministry come in for a break to hydrate and eat, and we start a conversation that we do not get to complete.

I really thank Brother Earle for his friendship, because he has been a sounding board for me to flush things out that are occurring in our current culture. I classify him as one of the "sons of Issachar," from 1 Chronicles 12:32, "men who understood the times, with knowledge of what Israel should do . . ." (NASB). Brother Earle, indeed, is one who knows "what time it is," and I would love to see him share the wisdom from his life and career with others who may not necessarily approach a subject without bias, but look at the truth for what it is, even if it disagrees with the majority.

Brother Earle has helped me with my sanity as I sometimes felt all alone on a matter and not wanting to compromise the truth of scripture. He has always been on God's side!

Rev. Bernard Snowden Jr.
Pastor of Family Life
Antioch Baptist

AMAZING FRIEND

Earle is an amazing friend with three exemplary qualities which we admire and respect. The first one is his strong faith and belief in our Lord and Savior, Jesus Christ. "Blessed is the man who trusts in the Lord, whose confidence is in Him," Jeremiah 17:7. I first met Earle at our Men's Retreat at Antioch Baptist Church (ABC) many years ago. One of the purposes of the retreat is to share God's Word and His amazing power to bless and shape our lives. Earle is a very faithful member of ABC, where he humbly serves in the parking ministry. During sunshine, rain, and other inclement weather conditions, you can depend on Earle to always be there. Earle, with his wife, Linda, served as commitment counselors for new members of ABC for many years. He continues to be a contributor to ABC Career Development Ministry and can be called upon to provide support for any of ABC's special needs in outreach to the community.

Earle's second exemplary quality is his integrity. His integrity is demonstrated by his professionalism, as seen in his outstanding career as an attorney and corporate executive at Comcast Corporation. I am forever grateful to Earle for hiring me to work as his human resources director at Comcast, when he was vice president and general manager at Comcast of Washington, DC. It was at Comcast that I observed his caring leadership, discipline, and honesty.

The third quality that we admire and respect about Earle is love for his family and friends. Earle demonstrates unconditional love to his lovely wife, Linda, his son Steve, his daughter-in-law Heather, his grandchildren, Ryan and Rachael, as well as to his sister, niece, and nephews.

He enjoys frequent family reunions in the USA, as well as travels to France to visit his relatives.

Earle and Linda are dependable, generous, and loving friends. They treat their family and friends to extravagant Christmas parties and summer cookouts, which are enjoyed and appreciated by all. They tell their friends the reasons they do it is because they care so deeply for family and friends and are glad we're in their life.

As a longtime true friend and brother in Christ, I was very proud to sponsor Earle into the Boulé (Sigma Pi Phi Fraternity, Beta Nu Boulé), where he contributes and shares his magnificent gifts for the betterment of mankind.

Curtis and Abby Taylor Sr.

A MAN OF CARING, SERVICE, AND CONVICTION

The number of men you find worshipping at most churches is not a large number. But when you find a man who is actively involved and committed to worship and supporting a church, and who stands his ground of convictions, you've found a true man of God. And, when that man is one who truly stands on and exercises his gGodly convictions, then that man will be sincerely revered, respected, and truly blessed.

CARING AND SERVICE

Earle is a very active member of Antioch Baptist Church, is a true servant of God, and truly serves the congregants of Antioch.

We don't know all of the ministries that Earle Jones is involved in at our church, but know that he is very active for at least two Sundays a month for some hours in the church's parking ministry, no matter the weather.

Being a parking attendant may not seem to be one that persons of Earle's stature and loft in the community and business world would aspire to do. It is a very demanding job that Earle and other parking ministry associates perform to delicately direct and assign parking spaces to church folks who often are late arriving for service. But seeing him on Sunday mornings warmly directing and assisting our worshipers to quickly find a parking space so they can hurriedly walk the distance over to the sanctuary, we see Earle doing this job with such selflessness, dedication, commitment, and satisfaction.

EXERCISING CONVICTION

Earle stands up for his convictions, no matter how delicate the subject may be. We've observed him whether it is dealing with people, discussing issues, and in all areas of interactions. For instance, it could be in the rights of the unborn, the racist treatment or abuse of people no matter their ethnicity, or the unfair treatment directed toward any persons. We've personally witnessed Earle exercise his convictions when we've been in his company. And we're sure he stands firmly rooted in his convictions at other times.

We truly believe that his stance upon his convictions definitely emanate from Earle being the Godly man that he is, from his commitment to being true and obedient to the Word of God, and from his love of the Lord.

We're also sure that Earle is compelled to stand firm because his parents taught him to do so. I did not know his parents. But Spike recalls when sitting in the choir loft at Earle's father's funeral, that comments expressed by Earle's late father's friends, coworkers, and family members, and even Earle himself, spoke of a father whose character was also of strong conviction, and who instilled such attributes to Earle. And, in reading his father's eulogy, we were informed of those attributes not only instilled by Earle's father, but also in what was read in the eulogy about Earle's late mother.

In addition, Earle chose very wisely in marrying a woman also of great conviction and character. His beautiful bride Linda Eatmon Jones no doubt underpins Earle's convictions and character.

My life has been truly enriched from meeting and knowing Earle and having him as a caring and true friend. He is one whom we wish we had as a brother for all of the years of our lives thus far.

Richard "Spike" Jones and Linda Stephens-Jones

THE QUIET SERVANT

Proverbs 11:25: "The liberal soul shall be made fat: and he that watered shall be watered also himself."

Rarely do we ever take the time to acknowledge or recognize those who go quietly through life serving God and making a difference in the lives of others. When Linda asked me if I would like to contribute to a book of essays about Earle, the first thought that ran through my mind was servant of God. After having worked with Earle on the Career Development Ministry and observing him as a friend and business colleague, I have developed a profound respect for his commitment and passion as a servant of God to his family and friends.

My first experience in meeting my good friend and Christian brother Earle was in the Men's Ministry at Antioch Baptist Church. Although Antioch has a large congregation, the ministries within the church provide members a wholesome atmosphere for Christian fellowship and networking within the Antioch family. As a new member of the church, I joined the Career Development Ministry and volunteered to lead this ministry. The purpose of this ministry was to provide a Christian experience that would inspire members of Antioch Baptist Church to reach their full career potential through counseling and mentoring. During my tenure within this ministry, I quickly learned that we could leverage Earle's talents and experiences as a corporate executive to help us build our program. Earle was an invaluable asset to the ministry who shared his experiences and resources as a business leader to help the program. Although Earle seems to be quiet and reserved, I learned that he is well connected and respected by his peers and associates in and out of Antioch Baptist Church. As a member of the ministry, we relied on his wisdom and intellect to guide and direct the ministry. During my tenure in this ministry, I cannot think of a time where he missed a meeting or commitment to the group. In addition to his commitment to God and the Career Development Ministry, I also gained an appreciation for Earl's devotion and love for his family and friends. He is truly a consummate leader, husband, father, and friend.

This became evident when I was invited to the first Christmas party that was hosted by Earle and Linda during the holiday season. I remember accepting the invitation, thinking that they would just have a small group of friends over for the Christmas party. My estimate of the number of attendees was probably off by a factor of 10 because what seemed to start out as a small gathering evolved into a major event. I was pleasantly surprised to learn that the large group consisted of Earle and Linda's immediate family, members of the neighborhood, and many Antioch friends. Each year that I have attended their party, I must commend the host and hostess for creating a *Homes and Garden* showcase that is filled with an abundance of love and joy during the holiday season. I realize that it takes a herculean effort and sound project plan to host a party of this magnitude, so my hat's off to Earle and Linda for making Christmas a special occasion for all to remember during the holiday season. They are a loving family, and more importantly, they give back that love to others in a Christian way.

Although I am no longer active in the Career Development Ministry, Earle continues to serve the church in the parking ministry. On any Sunday, he is the first person to greet you with a big smile and handshake. Rain or shine there has never been a time when he did not inquire about my family before leaving the parking lot to walk to the church. Even when Earle and Linda were faced with serious medical challenges, Earle always remained positive and upbeat, and most importantly, strong and faithful. They overcame one of the most difficult chapters of life with the support of God and their family and friends.

In closing, I am honored to acknowledge Earle as a servant of God, and a servant to his family and friends and wish him God's blessings as he continues through the next chapters of life.

Allen Sample

JUST EARLE—ANTIOCH BAPTIST CHURCH PARKING MINISTRY

I have the distinct honor and privilege of being a member of the Antioch Baptist Church Parking Ministry. Earle is also a member of this ministry. We serve together on this ministry several times a month, come rain or shine, in good weather or bad weather. On the Sundays or on special church events when we serve together, I'm always greeted by Earle with a firm handshake, a hug, and a genuine smile. Earle and I have often shared with each other and other members of the parking ministry our experiences growing up in our respective cities (Earle, Washington, DC and me, Philadelphia, Pa.). On our breaks between church services and during our impromptu discussions, Earle's conversation—**not boasting**—is often about his involvement of paying forward and giving back to his Washington, DC, community. I know that Earle is a member of an organization (SAFE) that serves underprivileged children in Washington, DC. I believe this organization provides these underprivileged children with tutors, mentors, and scholarships.

During one of our breaks between church services, the conversation centered on Washington, DC, and several of us mentioned that we know very little about the neighborhoods and history of the DC area. Earle volunteered to be our tour guide and take us to DC. Unfortunately, personal events precluded some of us from participating in the tour of DC. Hopefully, we can make the DC tour happen sometime this year.

When Earle talks about his family, he always has a smile on his face. He is very proud of how his son, Steve, turned his life over to Jesus Christ and is a youth minister. He shared with me that he has family who lives in France. He introduced me to his family from France when they visited him a few years ago. Most of all, Earle glows when the discussion is about his wife, Linda. Earle thanks everyone who takes the time to ask about her, her health, and who keep her in their prayers.

Earle is someone who never forgets where he came from. He is a Godly man, a devout and faithful family man, an honorable man, an educated man, and a sports enthusiast. Earle is well versed in all subject matters from politics, religion, education, community service, sports, entertainment, etc.

Arthur Coles, Antioch Baptist Church Parking Ministry

"NO ORDINARY MAN"

Despite his quiet and unassuming appearance and demeanor, Earle F. Jones is no ordinary, run-of-the-mill, average man. He has been, and continues to be, an achiever in all aspects of his life from high school, college, law school, and into his professional career where he has been in the forefront of the telecommunication industry's early expansion and more recent consolidation.

I did not know Earle while he was growing up a resident of Washington, DC, where he obtained his early education at a time when the nation was gradually desegregating public facilities and educational institutions, including in the nation's capital. Earle must have been an excellent student with a solid educational foundation inasmuch as his grades qualified him for enrollment at American University in 1965. After graduating from AU, he continued to pursue his education and expanded his horizon by enrolling in the University of California, Berkeley School of Law—a law school that is perennially ranked among the top 10 in the country. The Berkeley legal education set Earle on the path of success in the work world. Upon graduating, he proceeded to climb the corporate ladder with a stint in Denver, Colorado, before moving to Northern Virginia where I met him nearly 20 years ago.

While living in Virginia, he worked in Washington, DC, his hometown, for Cablevision which went through a series of acquisitions and was ultimately obtained by Comcast. Earle's professional success is demonstrated in the following job assignments which required great managerial skills and entailed increased responsibilities:

Vice President—General Manager, District Cablevision

Vice President—National Government Affairs, Comcast Eastern Division

Senior Director—Federal Government Affairs, Comcast

I have had the pleasure of socializing with Earle and his wife, Linda, for nearly 20 years, during which time we have enjoyed one another's company at the theater, in restaurants, and at other social events. However, the highlight of our time together was often spent in his home where he and his family were perfect hosts in regularly entertaining an eclectic collection of family and friends and treating them to a lavish spread of delicious food and beverages of all kinds. Earle and Linda's annual Christmas parties in their home are particularly special since the house, both inside and outside, is always festooned in an array of holiday decorations and lights and, of course, the entertainment is always unique and fun with lavish gifts awarded to contest winners.

Finally, while Earle has made significant professional achievements and has gained financial independence and despite his many affiliations, including membership in a prestigious fraternity of highly successful men, he has, nevertheless, chosen to serve his church as a member of the Parking Lot Ministry, a very humble position, which clearly demonstrates he has a servant's heart.

Earle F. Jones is a man of refinement and culture. He is a gentleman who has a deep and an abiding respect for men and women. He is a learned man who expresses himself with knowledge and intelligence. He is no ordinary man.

Leroy C. Latten

SERVICE "OUTSIDE" OF THE CHURCH

". . . just as the Son of Man did not come to be served, but to serve . . ." (Matthew 20:28)

Where does worship begin at Antioch Baptist Church in Fairfax, Virginia? Surprisingly, it actually begins in the church parking lots. Each and every Sunday, the Parking Lot Ministry, made up of dedicated volunteers, has the distinct opportunity to make a positive impression on our worshippers. This is the only ministry team that influences every person who drives onto our parking lots.

Earle Jones is one of those dedicated volunteers on Antioch's parking ministry. As a successful business executive, he could very easily choose to contribute to the church in many ways that would utilize his experiences in the legal, public policy, corporate management, boards and associations he serves on, etc., at times and places that would be more convenient for his busy schedule and inside, away from the sometimes harsh weather elements. Instead, he humbles himself and serves in the parking ministry.

I'm relatively new to the parking ministry so I have not served with Earle for a long time. However, for the time I've known him, he is the person who says out loud the good and wholesome things that everyone else is thinking but hesitant to state out loud.

Earle always has a smile on his face as he greets the drivers coming onto the lots. Regardless of the way they enter onto the lot, he beckons and waves to all as he is directing them to a parking space. He typically is scanning for people needing assistance to get them into spaces closest to the walkway.

Earle is someone who is serious about religion, family, and service, and is dedicated to giving his best effort to all of these things, which clearly demonstrates he has a servant's heart. We are grateful for his service and presence on the parking ministry and do enjoy his sharing his considerable wealth of knowledge.

God bless,
Brother Samuel Harris, Antioch Parking Ministry

A "GRACIOUS" MAN

As I was contemplating what I think of Earle Jones, *gracious* kept coming to my mind. Sometimes, people think of gracious as being a trait that one uses to describe women. Gracious can mean - courteous, polite, affable, good-natured, friendly, easygoing, and easy to talk to. That's the Earle I know.

I see this when I pull into the church parking lot on Sundays. When Earle recognizes me, he looks to see if he can locate a parking space that is as close to the sanctuary walkway as possible and politely guides me to it. His broad smile is always welcoming, and his easygoing manner makes it so easy to engage in conversation with him. I've never seen him in a cross mood; he's always friendly and good-natured, making sure he acknowledges you and what you have to say.

Another area I have great admiration and respect for in Earle is that of family loyalty. I am always so impressed with his recognition of his parents' life by putting a remembrance of their life each year in the *Washington Post*. He's been doing this since 1996 for his mother and 2008 for his father. How thoughtful, especially for a son, to be so consistently faithful to his parents' memory.

When I've encountered Earle at social events, like Steve's wedding or celebrations at their home, my husband and I feel so welcome, and Earle makes an attempt to ensure our comfort. An interaction with Earle is never about him—his humility is what you see.

At church, it's very easy to see his commitment to his faith in God. He now brings their grandchildren to church and is definitely the proud grandfather. You can depend on Earle because he is caring, and his concern for others and willingness to do what he can to help is so commendable. Today he can be a rare breed.

Blessings to a "gracious" and blessed man!!!

Mrs. Mary Alexander

A CHRISTIAN BROTHER AND FAMILY MAN

I've known Earle for many years. I met him through my soror, Linda. Earle, Linda, and I have often chatted before, during (the meet and greet) or after church. It wasn't until I asked Earle to serve on the parking ministry that I would come to know Earle, the man.

Earle's stature speaks volumes about his personality. His height presents a sense of strength. His soft steps reflect his quiet demeanor and his humility. His smile reveals a warmhearted and caring man. He loves his family and friends.

Earle is a man of few words, but the words he speaks are honest, trustworthy, and true. He neither boasts nor brags, but tells it like it is. When Earle makes a commitment, know that his word is his bond. There is no double talk or foolishness. He is a man of his word.

He serves faithfully and joyfully on the parking ministry, a thankless ministry at times, through the heat, rain, sleet, and snow. Regardless, Earle and the parking guys wave cars in and out of the parking lots of Antioch Baptist Church Sunday after Sunday. There are times when people aren't very cordial to the parking ministry, but Earle continues to smile. He takes things in stride as he takes the high road.

I am blessed, as are many others, to know Earle. I am thankful for him touching my life and being such a wonderful inspiration to me.

By His Love, Grace, and Mercy,
Keitha Johnson

EDUCATION

"Education is the most powerful weapon which you can use to change the world."
—Nelson Mandela

Knowledge is power—this insight is at least 4 centuries old, formulated by philosopher Francis Bacon during the Enlightenment period. His statement has lost nothing in terms of relevance and significance over the centuries. Knowledge is power, and education is the fundamental precondition for human condition, political development, democracy, and social justice. That can be seen each day in world affairs, but perhaps most importantly, in recent history through the Middle East instability that has impacted Western Europe and now the U.S. Education gives us knowledge of the world around us and changes it into something better. It develops in us a perspective of looking at life. It helps us build opinions and have points of view on things in life.

Earle often says that "education is the process of gaining information about the surrounding world while knowledge is something very different." Information cannot be converted into knowledge without education. Education makes us capable of interpreting things, among other things. It is not just about lessons in textbooks. It is about the lessons of life.

One of the best ways we can educate ourselves is to learn from our past. If you've known Earle for a while, you've probably heard him say, "*Those who don't know history are doomed to repeat it*" (Edmund Burke). Learning from our past provides us with a road map of the right and wrong way of doing things and gives us an idea of which way we should go if we experience new problems. Education does many wonderful things; it provides us opportunities, allows us to make informed decisions, improves society, and gives us the knowledge to discover new and wonderful inventions.

Earle values education and he is a student for life. He sees the many dimensions of acquiring knowledge and uses each facet to educate himself and the world around him constantly. He is a history buff. His appetite for reading books, online news, posts, blogs, and magazines is unparalleled to most. In 2005, I saved a sample of everything (except books) Earle read for that year. I made a 36x30 inch poster of just the names of the materials he read in an average month and presented it to him for his birthday. I had approximately 125 names on the poster, and this did *not* include books. He purchases and reads at least one book a month, sometimes more.

From a legacy of educators from administrative to postdoctoral work, master's and professional degrees, Earle learned early in life the power of knowledge acquired and the platform education provides to exploit that knowledge—the application of the knowledge. He has used it well and has earned and deserved the "sheepskins" to support his professional career.

A brief trip down Earle's educational memory lane follows: from Paul Junior High School to his graduation from Berkley School of Law. His lifetime of professional achievements, awards, recognitions, even trophies in music and sports in high school are quite a collection. They span civic, educational, business, religion, community, and professional areas. I would have to author a small book to present those. Maybe I can get one of our grandkids or great-nephews to do that.

PAUL JUNIOR HIGH

Junior High School Days—1959–1961
Paul Junior High (currently Paul Public Charter School)
5800 8th St NW, Washington, DC 20011

Paul's rooftop steeple is a neighborhood beacon, a symbol of welcome to the diverse students from across the District of Columbia who seek a program offering academic rigor in a character-building culture. Paul was awarded its charter status in 2000, becoming the first conversion public charter school in Washington, DC (and the only DC public school to charter conversion). Named after a pioneering DC educator, Edward Paul, and operating as a DC public school since 1930, Paul has a strong tradition of academic excellence and community involvement.

Earle attended Paul Junior High as a neighborhood middle school from 1959–1961. His mother taught at Garnet Patterson middle school, and when you have a parent teaching practically the same syllabus you are using at your school, it can be difficult to deny that you have homework or special projects to do. In addition to the academics, Earle started two things that would follow him thorough life—love for sports—as a spectator and player, basketball in particular—and love for all genres of music. He participated in numerous extracurricular activities both within the school setting and the community. He was a Boy Scout and an excellent swimmer. Earle did very well academically in junior high school, and his parents were a great part of that success—a family focused on educational excellence and a deep interest in music was born.

CALVIN COOLIDGE HIGH SCHOOL

High School Days—1961–1965
Calvin Coolidge High School
6315 5th St NW, Washington, DC 20011
Mascot: Colts
Colors: Orange and Grey

Coolidge was the first high school in the District to require physical education classes five periods per week. Athletics and physical activity have always been an important part of student growth and was a keen interest of Earle's from his early years. He was interested and followed all sports but enjoyed playing basketball the most. He played on the Colt's basketball team during high school and formed great relationships with his teammates that have lasted through the years.

Earle was a member of the "C" Club at Coolidge, one of the school's most exclusive clubs. Its members consisted only of boys who had been awarded a Coolidge "C." These letters were reserved for those who participated for given periods of time in Inter-High athletics.

Coolidge had an outstanding music program when Earle was in school. It was recognized as one of the premier music programs in DC, and so was the music director, Mr. Lyn McLain. Earle played flute in the 100-member marching band; 75-member orchestra; 20-member pit band playing the big band sounds; and the 15-member stage band playing Broadway musicals. Earle also served as the sergeant at arms for the music director to ensure student musicians adhered to the policies and guidelines. He honed his musical skills and was selected to play in the DC Youth Orchestra.

Earle was a very busy high school student with sports, music, church, Boy Scouts, and community service but was able to maintain his academic excellence. Graduating from Coolidge with many opportunities to attend various colleges, Earle decided on American University.

UNDERGRADUATE SCHOOL WAS SPENT AT AMERICAN UNIVERSITY IN WASHINGTON, DC, FROM 1965–1969.
4400 Massachusetts Ave. NW
Washington, DC 20016
Mascot: Clawed Z. Eagle
Colors: Green and White
Enrollment: 13,061 (2014)

American University (AU, or American) is a private research university in Washington, DC, affiliated with the United Methodist Church, although the university's curriculum is secular. AU was named the most politically active school in the nation in *The Princeton Review*'s annual survey of college students in 2008, 2010, and 2012. American University is especially known for promoting international understanding reflected in the diverse student body from more than 150 countries, the university's course offerings, the faculty's research, and from the regular presence of world leaders on its campus. The university has six schools, including the well-regarded School of International Service (SIS), currently ranked eighth in the world for its graduate programs and ninth in the world for its undergraduate program in International Affairs by Foreign Policy and the Washington College of Law.

Earle was a student athlete while at AU, playing forward on the AU men's basketball team. His major was sociology with a minor in history. While he did not live on campus, he participated in campus life and found history as one of his natural interests as well as a continuation of basketball. The diversity of cultures at AU planted seeds of exploring other countries in Earle.

LAW SCHOOL—UNIVERSITY OF CALIFORNIA, BERKLEY SCHOOL OF LAW

"God works wonders now and then;
Behold a lawyer, an honest man,"
— Benjamin Franklin

Upon graduation from AU, Earle took the Civil Service Examination and landed a job in Baltimore with the Federal

Highway Administration and worked in the Civil Rights Division for 5 years in Baltimore, Maryland. Knowing the world was larger than the corner he was currently in and feeling that yearn for more knowledge, Earle decided to take the Law School Admission Test (LSAT). He passed the LSAT the first time and headed to the University of California, Berkley School of Law. Everyone was surprised but pleasantly pleased because they knew he was destined for something bigger.

Berkeley School of Law is one of the nation's premier law schools, located at one of the world's great universities and in one of the most vibrant places. Berkeley Law is one of 14 schools and colleges at the University of California, Berkeley. It is consistently ranked as one of the top law schools in the nation.

The law school has produced leaders in law, government, and society, including Chief Justice of the United States Earl Warren, Secretary of State of the United States Dean Rusk, American civil rights activist Pauli Murray, California Supreme Court Justice Cruz Reynoso, president and founder of the Equal Justice Society Eva Paterson, United States Northern District of California Judge Thelton Henderson, and Attorney General of the United States Edwin Meese.

Earle's home was Berkley for 3 years. Although a long way from DC, he developed a law school family whose relationships still exist today. In the '70s, the enrollment of blacks at prestigious law schools was small. Earle found friendship and support from the other minorities enrolled. They studied together, marched and protested injustice together (the well-known Bakke case), partied (the "bump") together, and, supported each other. They symbolized some of the best minds from the areas of the U.S. they represented. Graduation was an exciting but somewhat sad time for a group that had been together as a family for a wonderful journey for 3 years.

After graduating from Berkley Law in 1977, Earle started a position in Denver working as an attorney with Holland & Hart, the largest Colorado-based law firm, with over a hundred attorneys in the Denver metropolitan area. The firm repeatedly leads the ranks of Colorado firms on the Best Lawyers in America list, Super Lawyers, Chambers & Partners, among other lists.

TRAVELING IS ANOTHER MEANS EARLE USES TO GAIN KNOWLEDGE.
Earle has traveled to every continent, except Antarctica and Australia, primarily on his personal time and expense. In Africa, he's traveled to Egypt, Ghana, Kenya, Nigeria, Ivory Coast, Senegal, South Africa, Zimbabwe, and the Republic of the Congo. In Asia, he visited Singapore, Philippines, Japan, India, and Indonesia. In Europe, his travels took him to France, Great Britain, and Germany. In South America, he and some colleagues traveled to Brazil to explore a personal business deal. Most of his travels in the U.S. have been part of his professional career; however, except Alaska and Hawaii, he's traveled to every state. Mexico and Canada are countries in North America he has visited, as well.

In 1993, Earle traveled to the Goree Island Slave Castle in Senegal, West Africa, to the Middle Passage area, and did the pilgrimage through the castle. It was constructed for the purpose of selling Africans in the Western World. Thus, the African Diaspora was born. Along the west coast of Africa, from Cameroon in the south to Senegal in the north, Europeans built some 60 forts/castles that served as trading posts. On the first leg of their trip, slave traders delivered goods from European ports to West African ones. On the "middle" leg called the Middle Passage, ship captains loaded their then-empty holds with slaves and transported them across the Atlantic Ocean and sold them to New World slave owners, who bought slaves to work their crops. A typical Atlantic crossing took 60–90 days but some lasted up to 4 months. During those crossings, at the height of the slave trade, between 1 and 2 million slaves died due to the inhumane conditions and treatment.

Many visitors to the Goree Island Slave Castle, where the slaves were held awaiting the ships, say they felt chills as they entered the castle and walked through the same ports the slaves did to enter those slave ships. Earle cites similar reactions. He visited a very special past in Goree Island, Senegal, that helped him to appreciate and experience his ancestral history and put it into a larger context of today.

In 1991, Earle made a 2-week pilgrimage to Egypt with the Institute of Karmic Guidance, whose goals are to disseminate and educate on ancient Egyptian history and metaphysics. Earle has a special passion for learning more about ancient Egyptian history. In our home today, he has a fascinating collection of Egyptian art, artifacts and books—the stories he can tell are countless. He is truly a student of history.

Whether Earle was traveling on the continent of Asia to Singapore, a country of lush tropical vegetation and amazing beaches, unforgettable rides, and a coexistence of different national traditions, or seeing some of the devastation of Subterranean Africa, or riding a camel as a means of transportation around the Great Pyramid of Giza, Egypt, or traveling to some of the cities of the U.S. greatly impacted by the economic downturn in industries that used to thrive (coal, agricultural, manufacturing, retail), Earle lives his mantra. *"He that would bring home the wealth of the Indies must carry the wealth of the Indies with him. So it is in travelling. A man must carry knowledge with him if he would bring home knowledge."* Samuel Johnson's quote is inscribed on the south face of Union Station in Washington, DC. Earle often says the same analogy can be made about education.

EDUCATION ESSAYS

- **Mr. Marcus Brown**, Past President, Calvin Coolidge Alumni Association

- **Mr. Carroll "Spyke" Henry**, President Smart Activities, Fitness, and Education

- **Mr. Lyn McClain**, Former Music Director, Coolidge HS

- **Ms. Phyllis Wells Blair**, Retired Community Services Volunteer, Metro DC area

- **Mr. Edward Riddick**

- **Mr. & Mrs. (Janice) Hilton Green**

- **Ms. Milele Archibald, Esq**., Retired Educator

- **Mrs. Rene Rambo-Rodgers, Esq.**, Human Resources Consultant, California Teachers Association

THE BIG MAN'S HEART

I am proud to write about Earle Jones. He has been a remarkable friend since our teenage years.

Earle & I attended both Paul JHS and Coolidge HS. It was not until high school that we bonded because we played on the basketball team together. Earle was one of the first "big men" (over 6 ft.) that played basketball in our class. He was a team player, always willing to help you on the court and off the court with homework. His heart and effort made him much bigger. Earle was a very popular guy throughout our high school career. Not only was he a very smart guy in the classroom and played sports—he also played in the band.

I was a football star that played basketball because the coach wanted me to stay in shape. I know firsthand that a few guys envied Earle because of his skills, talent, and heart. To this day, I do not know if Earle knew who the guys were that envied him or if he cared, because he never changed his character or personality.

Although our teams never played for a championship, the relationship we developed made me a stronger person. Back then, we had a saying, "It is not whether you win or lose—it's how you play the game." That meant you always want to do your best—give it your all—ALWAYS. Earle embodied that most of all. He was able to help us understand what teaming really meant.

SENIOR YEAR

During our senior year of high school I had a career-ending knee surgery (football) that wiped out several scholarship offers. By the grace of God, the head football coach appointed me the Junior Varsity (JV) coach, which started my coaching career at the age of 17, working with youth.

As the JV coach, I met with quite a few students and athletes. Several of them always mentioned how they wished they had Earle's work ethics, skills, and talent.

Upon graduating from high school, Earle went to American University and subsequently out West to law school. We lost touch with each other during those years, but our friendship was cemented from the early years at Paul and Coolidge.

SEVERAL YEARS LATER

Earle returned home to take care of his ailing parents in the early '90s. I had started a community nonprofit sports development organization, working with youth and young adults, also as a Certified Tennis Teaching Professional.

Our paths crossed again. We met at a fundraising event, and I invited Earle to attend a meeting of a community nonprofit I started, Smart Activities for Fitness and Education (SAFE). We were looking for board members and fund-development volunteers. After hearing our goals for community kids who did not have the opportunity to learn tennis and who needed a mentor while in school, Earle decide to join our board of directors.

Just like in high school, his heart opened to our situation and the kids we supported. A few meetings later, Earle was nominated as chairman of the board. Everyone could see his leadership abilities, but more important, his "teaming" approach to leading. He accepted the position, and SAFE has grown ever since.

Looking back over the years, I now see why/how they say college is very important. However, I also think it is high school where you set the stage for life. Earle was an outstanding leader in high school and continues to be one today.

Carroll "Spyke" Henry (high school classmate)

REDISCOVERED CLASSMATE

The nature of youth is *not* to realize and recognize who and what you are surrounded by. In high school, I didn't really know Earle. There was never any communication. I'd see him in passing and thought of him as a quiet and studious guy.

Aside from both of us being graduates of Calvin Coolidge and on the alumni committee, about 10 years ago, I later found we also share common community interests and became affiliated with many community organizations for the betterment of African Americans, and as a result, developed a great friendship. We are both affiliated with the Congressional Black Caucus, Political Action Committee, and Smart Activities for Fitness and Education (SAFE). Who would have known?

At the Greater Washington Urban League (GWUL), Earle was on the board of directors and I worked with a development company that provided homes for first-time homebuyers, and many of the purchasers were referred by GWUL.

After rediscovering my classmate, a good relationship started, and I began to really appreciate his friendship. He and Linda have welcomed me into their home, and I have called on him when I needed help at his senior level of management at Comcast and received it immediately.

Earle is a genuinely nice person; he always brings a smile. I'm glad to call him friend.

Phyllis Wells Blair (High school classmate)

THE FLUTE PLAYER

I saw Earle Jones a couple of years ago at a high school reunion in Washington, DC. I don't think I had seen Earle since he graduated from Coolidge. I had heard from others that he had gone on to college and law school and was doing well in his career.

Earle was a music student at Coolidge, playing the flute in several music groups I conducted. He was a very good flute player and a much-disciplined music student. Earle got along with all musicians, which can be difficult at a young age. He was my sergeant in the military band—his responsibilities included being in charge of discipline for all music students across all music groups. Earle made sure they showed up on time and had with them the items they needed for a performance or trip. He served in this role while he was in high school and did it exceptionally well.

Coolidge High School had the reputation for having one of the best music programs and bands in DC when Earle was in school. Earle belonged to the 100-member marching band, 75-member orchestra, 20-member pit band playing the big band sounds, and the 15-member stage band playing Broadway musicals. In addition, Earle played with the DC Youth Orchestra with student musicians from all over the city.

The stage band performed Broadway musicals each year, such as *Guys and Dolls, Pajama Game,* etc. for extraordinarily large audiences. The orchestra traveled and performed in many competitions such as at Duquesne University in Pittsburg, Pennsylvania, where the orchestra received an outstanding award for musical excellence.

Earle's father served on The Friends of DC Youth Orchestra board which supported the various music groups, and his tenure extended after Earle graduated from high school. Earle was indeed a dedicated musician, and I enjoyed the time he performed in all four music groups under my direction.

Mr. Lyn McClain
Former Music Director, Coolidge High School

CLASSMATES AGAIN

As a student at Coolidge High School between 1962–1965, I remember seeing Earle walking through the halls. I don't remember if I ever spoke to him socially, but we did take some classes together, and we may have conversed in the classroom. Since Earle was a member of the varsity basketball team, he was someone I looked up to. Little did I know that 50 years later, I would be able to count on him any time our class was getting together or working on some type of fundraiser.

Each year when the Calvin Coolidge Alumni Association meets for our annual scholarship breakfast, Earle is always one of the first to contact me to reserve his seat. Earle has also been a regular contributor to our class scholarship fund. A few years ago, I had a nephew seeking employment, so I called Earle for some guidance, and he was there to offer any assistance he could give.

Earle is a quiet, private person—but he is there for his friends and classmates when they need him.

Congratulations, Earle, and may we continue this special friendship for many years to come.

Marcus Brown (High school classmate)
Past president, Calvin Coolidge Alumni Association

MEMBER OF OUTSTANIDNG MUSIC PROGRAM

Earle played the flute in all of the four music bands at Coolidge High School—the marching, orchestra, stage, and show pit bands. All of the bands were under the direction of Mr. Lyn McClain and had the reputation of being part of the best music program in the DC public schools for many years. The stage band was invited to perform at the DC premiere of three major motion pictures. The band performed at the premiere of the film *The Longest Day* for Montgomery County Committee for a Democratic Congress at the Ontario Theater. The band performed *The Longest Day* theme song composed by Maurice Jarre. Actor/singer Paul Anka and Maurice Jarre were in attendance.

The Stay-in-School Fund Benefit, chaired by realtor Ms. Flaxie Pinkett, invited the band to perform at the premiere of *Charade* in 1963 and *Topkapi* in 1964. Mr. Gray Grant, the film's star and producer, made a special appearance to support the benefit, and Ms. Ella Fitzgerald performed prior to the film's viewing. In 1964, Mr. Sammy Davis Jr. and Mr. Bob Newhart performed prior to the screening of the film. These screenings were held at the Palace Theater in DC.

In each of these performances, the stage band members received considerable accolades for our outstanding musical performances, especially from high school students. It not only gave our musical students the opportunity to meet celebrities, but it increased the exposure of the Coolidge music program for community and city support.

John Mercer (Coolidge High classmate and band member)

ALWAYS A GENTLEMAN

Earle grew up on Somerset Street in NW Washington as did Janice. He was always very kind to her mother. Earle was a gentleman, in school and outside of school. His demeanor was always very respectful to everyone. He was reserved and well thought of by his peers. In seeing him many years later, I can say he is the same as he was back in high school—a good guy.

Both Hilton and I went to Coolidge High School, and Hilton played in the band with Earle. His focus was very much into the music, and he participated in all of the four bands of the school. Earle also served as the sergeant at arms for the music director. He was very serious about music and always displayed a calm and serious demeanor.

Janis and Hilton Greene Sr. (High school classmates)

A GENUINELY NICE PERSON

There can be many definitions for *nice*, and sometimes, it seems a bit commonplace to say that about a person; however, Earle was "pleasant—nice, kindhearted—nice, and polite—nice." Overall, he respected people, regardless of who they were.

I was on the basketball team and in the band with Earle. He was also very active in many sports. His dedication and commitment to each was commendable. Regardless of how good he was, he always did his best or gave it his best. In seeing him several times at reunions over the past 10 years, this is a trait that Earle has taken into adulthood and in every aspect of his life. He has performed very well professionally and has very close family relationships.

One of the things I recall about Earle in high school, when sitting idle, Earle had an odd habit of taking one hand and patting it into the other (knuckle to palm) when deep in thought. Perhaps that was his way of blotting out the outside noise while thinking.

Edward Reddick (High school classmate)

GREAT SECTION 2 CLASSMATE

I was fortunate to have Earle Jones in my section for law school. At the time we went, the entering first-year class was divided into two sections. Earle, John Whitehead, and I were all in the same section; we became fast friends and running buddies since we were all single and fancy free. Being in the same section meant we had all of our first-year classes together, except for one small lecture class. EJ was the steady one of the three of us—very grounded and supportive. I was the Los Angeles lost soul, and John was still identifying with West Oakland, his home. Although we all experienced the trials and tribulations of being first-year black law students, we very supportive of one another, whether it be studying or relationship woes (and believe you me, we *all* experienced something). But we had time to protest Bakke (a law class trying to eliminate affirmative action) and party at different classes (first-, second-, or third-year) and events, dancing the night away. EJ was one "mean" bump partner. He *loved* that dance.

Can't actually remember what year we were in, but I had just washed and rolled my hair in the gigantic hair rollers of the time. I was getting ready to sit under the hair dryer when Earle called and said, "Let's go to Sausalito." I said I couldn't because obviously I had to dry my hair. Well, Earle protested and said he needed to get out, and he needed some company. He had always been there for me, and so, I agreed to go. But that meant I couldn't dry my hair. So alas, Earle came to get me, and I, if you can believe, hopped in the grand old Charger, curlers and all, and off we went to Sausalito. I remember going over the Richmond/San Rafael Bridge. This was completely strange to me, because the only way I had ever gone to Sausalito was through San Francisco, over the Golden Gate Bridge. But I didn't say a word (which was definitely strange for me because I'm an L.A. driver, and we *always* want to know the "ins and outs" of where we are going). But I could tell, Earle just wanted to cruise, needed some company, and time to hang out. So we arrived, got out of the car, and started walking up and down the tourist-filled streets, checking out the sights. And then, of all things, along down the street comes this fine brother headed in our direction. I'm basically in a panic because I have the humongous curlers in my hair and looked terrible. I then started saying, "Oh, Earle, how could I have come out looking like this, in this area of all places?" I wanted to hide under a rock right then and there. But wonderful, gracious Earle assured me, no need to worry; it was okay. I didn't look that bad (nice white lie, EJ J)!!! So he and I just kept hanging out the rest of the afternoon. I just remember it was such a pleasant and beautiful day, with good company, and that he was with a true friend.

The other thing that really stands out had to do with our Administrative Law class during our second year. Earle, John, and I were all in the same study group (all black), which included both second- and third-year students. The class was probably one of the most boring subjects I took in law school. So the group decided that each of us would read a chapter and make a complete outline of it. Then, all of the outlines would be combined into one document for us each to use and study from. Well, unfortunately, John didn't complete his part. So the third-year student, who was the lead of the study group, told John he couldn't have the combined outline to study from for our final because he didn't complete his part. John was furious and things were headed to really get out of hand. But Earle, being more mature, pragmatic, and weighing the situation at hand, decided to de-escalate it. He was so unselfish and shared the final document. Not sure if he gave John his copy or made a copy for him, but he made sure he had the material. From his perspective, although John hadn't contributed as he should have, it was more important to support a "fellow brother" so he could pass the exam, then to punish him for not doing what he was supposed to do. Let's just say that

Earle made sure the situation didn't become volatile, because it was definitely headed that way; after all, this was the late '70s, and there was still a lot of radicalism around.

They don't make them like Earle any more. He truly is a special and wonderful person—very unselfish. Success has never gone to his head. You could tell him a secret in confidence, and you never feared it would be shared with others. And on that note, he was one heck of a private man himself as he didn't put his personal business out in the street either. I am honored to have had the opportunity to spend 3 years in law school with Earle. We did stay in touch for a number of years while he lived in Denver, but over the years, as it happens, you look up and you're just not in touch like you used to be. But even so, Earle, you will always hold a very special place in my heart.

René Rambo-Rodgers, Classmate, Class of 1977
University of California, Berkeley School of Law

BOALT HALL'S DANCING MACHINE

Who knew Earle Jones would outdance everybody on the dance floor doing the "bump" with his partner, Milele!

That was Earle Jones in between joining fellow law school classmates in study groups and picket lines and doing other necessary things like sleeping, eating, going to class, and playing basketball. Although we worked hard, what I most remember about Earle, my friend, my dance buddy, was our love for "the bump." We hit the dance floor with the "bump," bumping hips, shoulders, butts, knees, heads, elbows, calves, arms—to any and every song played. And we were good!

We danced to The O'Jays, "Love Train," The Temptations, "For the Love of Money," Aretha's, "House That Jack Built," The Commodores, "Brick House," and James Brown's, "The Big Payback." We bumped with Al Green, Marvin Gaye, Diana Ross, Earth, Wind and Fire, Kool and the Gang, Stevie, Otis, Gladys, Barry, Isleys, Four Tops, Parliament, and Booker T—you name the song, we bumped!

I don't know how I would've made it through law school without the fun times we had at our parties while navigating the travails of constitutional law, civil procedure, estates, property law, torts, contracts, evidence, remedies, and preparing for the mighty bar exam.

We graduated 40 years ago this year. I haven't seen my bump partner since then. But we will always be the bump champs! Thanks for the memories, my friend.

Milele Archibald, Classmate, Class of 1977
University of California, Berkeley School of Law

EDUCATION PHOTOS

The "C" Club—athletes who lettered in sports awarded school

Senior Picture

Senior Band and Concert

Varsity Basketball Team

Freshmen Basketball Team

Earle and Teammates at Practice

Camaraderie and Fun Study Groups

Protesting Injustice

LAW SCHOOL GRADUATION—JUNE 1977

TRAVELING IN EGYPT

THE WORLD OF
WORK

"The only place success comes before work is in the dictionary."
—Vince Lombardi

After law school, Earle moved to Denver in 1977 to work for Holland and Hart. The law firm is still the largest Colorado-based law firm, with more than 200 attorneys in the Denver metropolitan area. The firm repeatedly leads the ranks of Colorado firms on the Best Lawyers in America list, Super Lawyers, Chambers & Partners, among other lists. With a full complement of corporate and litigation legal services and an advanced trial preparation center and mock trial room, Earle was able to develop a solid foundation in the corporate legal world. Earle's projects and cases were in the then growing energy industry.

Earle lived and worked in Denver from 1977–1994. After Holland and Hart, Earle worked for the Regional Transportation District (RTD) as one of their legal representatives. The RTD is the regional authority operating public transit services in eight of the 12 counties in the Denver-Aurora-Boulder Combined Statistical Area in Colorado. At the RTD, Earle established many relationships in the legal and business arenas, as well as many lasting friendships. Earle benefitted from the exposure and knowledge he gained by working with experienced litigators. He found this knowledge most helpful throughout his career in understanding the nexus between the business world, government, and legal.

One of the "rites of passages" for a lawyer is to hang your own shingle. Earle spent a few years in private practice with a partner in Denver. The firm provided legal services primarily in real estate, wills, trusts, and family law. He was recommended by one of the then Colorado Supreme Court Justices to serve on the Judicial Ethics Advisory Board as the Ethnics Counselor for the Colorado lawyers. Earle served in that capacity for 2 years. During those years, he also worked as an adjunct law professor at the University of Denver, teaching business writing. He excelled in writing during high school, undergraduate, and law school. Earle attributes his successful writing skills to the days he sat at the dining-room table under the instruction of the best writer he knew . . . his mother.

Earle maintained active membership in the National Bar Association while working directly in the law field in Denver. The "Negro Bar Association," later called the National Bar Association (NBA), was founded after some of the National Bar Association founders were denied membership in the American Bar Association. Earle worked tirelessly, with the chair of the Denver NBA to make Denver the host city for the 1986 NBA National Convention, a prize for any city. The group was successful, as was the convention, with one of the largest number of attendees during that time. Today, the NBA is still the nation's oldest and largest national association of predominantly African American lawyers, judges, educators, and law students. It has 84 affiliate chapters throughout the United States and affiliations in Canada, the United Kingdom, Africa, Morocco, and the Caribbean. It represents a professional network of more than 60,000 lawyers, judges, educators, and law students.

With over 17 years of legal experience with a large prestigious law firm, in private practice, serving in many other legal roles (president of the Sam Cary Bar Association, NBA National Conference Committee), and city-level government relations on policy-related issues, Earle became interested in the start-up of the young, budding, cable telecommunications industry. That interest moved him to the Washington, DC, metro area and has lasted more than 25 years.

His first position in cable was with Tele-Communications Inc. ("TCI") in Denver in 1989, where he served as division director for government affairs for 5 years. From 1994–1997, Earle was TCI's FCC Washington Counsel. He was in this position when the historic 1996 Telecom Act was passed. From 1997–1998, he served as TCI's Mid-Atlantic director of government affairs, a region covering five states.

From 1998 until 2001, Earle was the general manager for Washington, DC's, District Cablevision and led that system through three ownership changes. Those ownership changes included the acquisition of TCI by AT&T in 1999, the buyout of local partner Bob Johnson by AT&T in 1999, and the acquisition of District Cablevision from AT&T by Comcast in January 2001. Here, Earle learned the nuts and bolts of cable operations that still serve him well today.

From 2001 to 2008, Earle returned to a policy role with the responsibility of overseeing first the Atlantic Division, and then, after their consolidation, the Eastern Division group's relationships with their respective federal elected officials. Earle was vice president of government affairs for Comcast's Eastern Division which served approximately 5 million customers in Delaware, Maryland, Pennsylvania, New Jersey, Virginia, and West Virginia. As a result, Earle's relationships with elected officials on Capitol Hill grew and naturally expanded into more of a public policy role for the corporation.

In January 2009, Earle joined Comcast Corporation's Washington Federal Government Affairs office team that successfully obtained federal regulatory approval for the Comcast/General Electric acquisition of NBCUniversal in January 2011.

In 2014, Earle was recognized by Lawyers of Color as one the nation's 50 Top Lobbyists and Influencers.

Networking, relationship building, and financial prudence are other keys to Earle's successful career. He stresses them to the young people he mentors and teaches them how to network and to invest for their future. They all have become successful using his suggestions. Earle has what appears to be a gazillion contacts. He has business cards from all over the world and carries two mobile phones. However, his humility is what people see first, and I think that's how he makes such lasting impressions—having a name like Earle Jones also helps with his distinguished baritone voice.

Earle has worked for Comcast Corporation since 1999 and appreciates the type of company it is—family owned and operated and philanthropic with a keen sense for the needs of the underserved. Comcast Corporation is a global media and technology company with two primary businesses, Comcast Cable and NBCUniversal. Earle worked on the Comcast Cable side of the business for 5 years as a general manager and government affairs VP. Comcast Cable is one of the nation's largest video, high-speed Internet, and phone providers to residential customers under the XFINITY brand and also provides these services to businesses. NBCUniversal operates news, entertainment, and sports cable networks, the NBC and Telemundo broadcast networks, television production operations, and television station groups, Universal Pictures, and Universal Parks and Resorts. Comcast employs thousands of employees but strives to maintain services focused on the needs of its employees.

Earle has always believed in goal setting and reflection—nothing is sporadic; his movements are well thought out in planning career moves. He values discipline and consistency; commitment to his organization;

reliability and consistency in his work products; loyalty to staff; dependability (his word is his bond); and, timeliness. Two quotes he lives by are "the early bird gets the worm" and "time and tide for no man waits; be quick, prompt, or be too late." In his career and personal life, Earle is a risk taker but disciplined in approach. He believes you do not have to see the entire staircase to take the first step.

WORK ESSAYS

- **Mr. Harry Alford**, President, National Black Chamber of Commerce

- **Mr. David Breidinger**, Senior Vice President, Government Affairs, Comcast Northeast Division

- **Mr. Rudy Brioche**, Global Public Policy, Comcast Corporation

- **Mr. David Cohen**, Senior Executive & Vice President & Chief Diversity Officer, Comcast Corporation

- **Mr. Wiley Daniel**, Senior United States District Judge, U.S. District Court, Denver, Colorado

- **Mrs. Charisse Lille**, Vice President Community Investment, Comcast Corporation

- **Mr. Sean Looney**, Vice President, State Government Affairs, Maryland, Comcast NBCUniversal

- **Ms. Melissa Maxfield**, Senior Vice President for Federal Government Affairs, Comcast Corporation

- **Mr. Robert Omberg**, Vice President, State Government Affairs, Virginia, Comcast NBCUniversal

- **Ms. Eldean Penn**, Administrative Assistant, Federal Government Affairs, Comcast Corporation

- **Mr. Bret Perkins**, Vice President, External and Government Affairs, Comcast Corporation

- **Mrs. Veronica Santos-Mazzuchi**, Manager, Community Investment, Comcast Beltway Region

- **Ms. Jennifer Stewart, Ph.D.**, President, Stewart Strategies & Solutions, LLC

- **Ms. Lelia True**, Comcast Cable

- **Ms. Sheila Willard**, Recently Retired, Former SVP of Local Media Development, Comcast Cable

- **Mr. Anthony (Tony) Williams**, Senior Director Government and External Affairs, Comcast Corporation

THE EARL(E) OF JONES

Earle's leadership, his presence, his credibility, and his stature all have played a central role in building Comcast's reputation on Capitol Hill. He is truly viewed as "royalty" by members of Congress and their staff.

In 2002, when Comcast acquired AT&T Broadband, Comcast moved into a leadership role in representing the cable industry's interests and the company's interests, in Washington, DC. At the same time, Comcast's footprint expanded from a distinct minority of the Congress to covering most of the Congress, either because of our expanded geographic footprint or because of our need to reach out to leadership and leading members of Congress. One of the central strategies developed was an aggressive program to create relationships with all of the diversity caucuses, including the Congressional Black Caucus ("CBC").

In view of this strategy, we asked Earle to transition from a field-based government affairs role to join our growing Washington office and to take the lead in developing relationships with the CBC. Earle readily agreed, and both developed a strategy for outreach to all members of the CBC, and then executed flawlessly on that strategy. Today, Comcast enjoys a very strong relationship with the CBC, covering members both within the Comcast footprint and outside our footprint. And much of that relationship is due to Earle's personal relationships with members of the CBC. He is universally respected—and beloved—by members and staff.

While professionally, Earle has earned the royal title of Earl(e), his qualities as a person and human being have been even more important to the company. He is widely viewed as one of the most decent human beings anyone has ever met. And he has played a central role in building a positive and constructive culture in the Washington office.

Comcast benefits from a remarkable government affairs team. And in many ways, Earle Jones has been the heart and soul of that team. It is hard to imagine how the Washington government affairs function would have developed without Earle's leadership and participation.

David L. Cohen
Senior Executive
Vice President & Chief Diversity Officer
Comcast Corporation

"CAPTAIN EARLE"
With the distinctive voice and loyal heart

Earle has worked on my team for 8 years. Before working directly on the federal GA team, Earle and I worked together from his position in Comcast's Eastern Division. I have known Earle all of the 13 years I have been at Comcast. During that time, we have seen the company grow in ways we would not have ever imagined. Throughout this time, Earle has been one of the pillars for me. Having come from many years in the cable industry, he plays the role of the teacher, confidant, friend, and advisor on how cable systems operate. My team would not be complete without his knowledge, history of the company and industry, and his understanding of how our systems operate in a competitive market. He is our guiding light.

From the integration of AT&T Broadband to the NBCU acquisition, the Verizon Spectrum deal, the TWC deal, and many legislative battles on the Hill, Earle has played the role of elder statesman to my team on how we understand the operational changes, what they actually mean for our business, and how we operate as a team. We live in a sea of change, and Earle serves as our guidepost and lighthouse shedding wisdom.

He is a Captain, a leader, and, yes, battle-tested. Earle has been through the sharpest waters and has helped keep our collective boat steady and stay afloat. He is trusted and loved and that is felt and by every interaction he has with his members, their staff, and numerous national leaders who treat him with reverence.

My team would not be a team without Earle. He is always there for us. His steady hand keeps us from getting too close to the rocks, and he always steers us to the light.

Melissa Maxfield, Senior Vice President
Federal Government Affairs
Comcast NBCUniversal

EARLE "THE TOUCHSTONE" JONES

I've known Earle since I started with the company over 14 years ago. He has remained a selfless professional who has been an advocate for the company and a caring colleague. In a tough town and profession, Earle has been effective without losing his decency.

Earle has seen a lot in his time with the company. Having helped get approval for the AT&T Broadband transaction, he had the great experience of making the union work . . . and that all began with Horse Whispering with Sheila at Miraval . . . (an inside joke for a small handful of folks). Most who know him now but don't know his history might not imagine him hanging out with local regulators at NATOA. But Earle has always been comfortable around all kinds of people, whether walking through city halls or through the halls of Congress. In fact, it's that versatility that, in part, opened up the door for the latest stage in his career. As a leader in the previous Mid-Atlantic Division of the company, though his primary role was local and state government affairs, many came to rely on him for his relationships with the congressional delegation from his division.

Though based in Philadelphia, I am a frequent visitor to the DC office. Like Earle, I am an early riser and like being at my desk before most, which means, when I am in DC, I can always count on a quick good morning conversation with him. He is always diligent about checking in on me, and even more important, to me, he is always kind to ask about my father.

Earle is a class act all around. Comcast and the cable industry continue to benefit from his steadfast and loyal service. His colleagues benefit from having someone around who genuinely cares about the people with whom he works and interacts.

Bret Perkins, Vice President
External and Government Affairs
Comcast Corporation

THE "READY, STEADY" EARLE JONES

In my 25-year tenure, I have been engaged in strategy and advocacy with many lobbyists. Some were geniuses in their craft. Many were zealots pushing toward a goal, whether it was wrong or right. They were given a mission and by "hook or crook," they were going to achieve that mission. Earle is of another code. He will examine my belief and attitude about a specific subject or position. If that position is consistent with his, then we can proceed with a strategy and a definition of success. From there, the mission is formed, and we enact our battle plan. Far more times than not, we have been victorious.

We have had many discussions on "Politics versus Good Judgment." Earle has consistently shown that good judgment trumps politics. This attitude and posture is a matter of integrity. He never has a negative gesture or position. He figures out what is the right thing to do for his company and the national economy. It's like he stops to figure out . . . "What would Jesus do?"

Earle has an impressive résumé. You have to pull this out of him, piece by piece. There is not a hint of conceit in this man.

He is also a very courageous person. There have been health challenges with him and his family, but none of that has put him off his game. His faith gets him and his family through those obstacles. God is great, and Earle Jones firmly believes that.

The above is why I love this guy so. It's why I have written and submitted testimony to the FCC from my hospital bed. If it is important to Earle, I must complete the mission. If Earle says we must take "the hill," then the hill will be taken.

Work ethic, faith, and love of family and country is what Earle Jones is all about. I am certain that when his "name is called," St. Peter will say, "Job well done."

Harry C. Alford, President
National Black Chamber of Commerce

A WARM WELCOME

They say you can never go home again, but I was doing just that. It was 2007; I'd joined Comcast, moved to Philadelphia, and was now back in DC visiting Comcast's DC offices to meet the federal government affairs team.

This DC was different from the one I'd inhabited before. Gone were the classrooms and classmates I knew as a boy; the familiar faces and comradely of other Hill staffers; and the community leaders, activists, and organizers I knew as a candidate. Their color, youth, exuberance, and community replaced by corporate environment that was populated by older, whiter, corporate faces who worked quietly and expertly in suits and ties ensconced within offices and behind closed doors.

I was nervous. I was intimidated. This DC felt like anywhere but home.

This was the first time I met Earle Jones. Tall, black, and refined, Earle spoke with a knowing majesty that conveyed friendliness. His words closing the distance between us, making me feel immediately comfortable and welcoming me home. Earle reminded me that despite my differences, I was here because I too possessed expertise, had something to offer, and would be successful in this new corporate environment.

Earle has been a constant and reaffirming presence in my work life since then. As a friend, colleague, and mentor, few people have had the impact on my growth and development at Comcast as Earle Jones. Earle, quite simply, is a Pearl.

Antonio (Tony) Williams, Senior Director
Government and External Affairs
Comcast Corporation

THE GENTLE GIANT WITH THE BIG HEART AND LOTS OF FAMOUS FRIENDS

"I've learned that people will forget what you said, people will forget what you did,
but people will never forget how you made them feel."
—Maya Angelou

Earle Jones and I became fast friends when I joined Comcast. We both have an affinity for the law, public policy, and Comcast. We both have a fascination with politics. We both have a deep love of family. I have been privileged to have Earle as a friend, mentor, and role model since joining Comcast. I have such respect for his experience and his awesome academic credentials. He is a very tall man, with a very gentle soul. And he has many famous friends!

During the decade that I have been at Comcast, I have always attended the annual Congressional Black Caucus Legislative Weekend. There is always a receiving line around Earle! The members of Congress are genuinely pleased to see him, and there are warm exchanges and bear hugs. It is always great to see the high regard in which he is held by our elected officials. Earle is a seasoned professional who represents Comcast with distinction.

When Linda was having her health challenges, Earle did not give me many details. But he was clearly worried and deeply concerned about her treatment and recovery. When he gave me the great news that Linda was recovered and doing really well, he radiated joy. It was wonderful to see him so happy. Linda is a blessing to Earle, and Earle is a blessing to Linda.

To quote my shero, Dr. Angelou, I will never forget how Earle made me feel from the very first time I encountered him. He made me feel like a sister, a friend, a valued addition to his circle of friends. I feel the same about him. He is my brother and my friend. I am so blessed that he is in my circle of friends.

I am honored to be a part of this celebration of your wonderful life, Earle. Congratulations and God speed!

Charisse R. Lillie, Vice President
Community Investment
Comcast Corporation

"BROTHER EARLE"—THE EPITOME OF NOBILITY

It is my immense honor to celebrate Brother Earle—Role Model, Consigliere, Brother.

I call Earle "Brother Earle" because anyone with the baritone voice of James Earl Jones, the commanding stature of Paul Robeson, and the towering presence of Kareem Abdul-Jabbar, is deserving of a title of nobility. When I was growing up in Brooklyn and going to high school in Harlem, I learned the title of "Brother" is noble and reserved for a man who has earned or can demand respect. It did not take me long, after spending some time with Brother Earle, to realize that he was deserving of this title, not only because of his physical attributes, but, more importantly, because of what lies in his heart: humility and an abiding love and unyielding commitment to his wife, family, and faith.

To have an opportunity to work with and learn from someone like Brother Earle in corporate America is truly a blessing. Corporate America has its unique challenges for a black man, but it's one of the best places to be when you're fortunate to work for an entrepreneurial company in a highly dynamic and competitive industry, and there's someone you inherently connect to and can trust, appreciate, and emulate. For me, Brother Earle is that person.

On many days, the most stress-free part of my workday is having coffee with Brother Earle early in the mornings before many of our colleagues get into the office. Never disappointing, he is always the first one in the office, masterfully ready to take on the day and its unpredictability. Brother Earle's wide range of experiences on the business, operational, and policy sides of Comcast have given him an impressive 360-degree understanding of the information, communications, and technology sector, particularly the cable industry. This, and the genuinely good person he is, makes Brother Earle the perfect person with whom I want to discuss new ideas and let my guard down, and from whom I seek advice and guidance.

I am truly blessed and eternally grateful to have a special place in my heart for Brother Earle, *the epitome of nobility*.

Rudy N. Brioché
Global Public Policy
Comcast Corporation

LOYAL FRIEND

In the summer of 1977, Earle Jones and I arrived in Denver and began a bond, fellowship, and friendship that has spanned almost 30 years. Earle had just graduated from law school, and I had just relocated to Denver from 6 years of practice in Detroit, Michigan. Earle and I got acquainted because we were African American lawyers who practiced at large Seventeenth Street, Denver law firms, and we immediately sensed a kindred spirit one for the other as we spent time together. One of our first joint activities was participation in Sam Cary Bar Association, Colorado's association of black attorneys. Earle was elected president of Sam Cary in 1980, and I followed him as president in 1981. During my tenure as president, the National Bar Association (NBA) awarded to Sam Cary Bar Association the honor of hosting the annual convention of the NBA in 1986. Between 1981 and 1986, Sam Cary formed many committees to ensure that the first ever NBA Convention to be held in Denver would be an outstanding success.

Leading up to the NBA Convention that took place in the summer of 1986, I served as chair of Sam Cary's Convention Planning Committee and Earle was our treasurer, financial secretary, and the person who was responsible for all money and budget management issues. Earle's contributions to the success of the conclave were substantial. As he exhibited with all the projects we worked on over the years, Earle's loyalty, reliability, and guidance were on display and much appreciated. For many years following the conclusion of the NBA's 1986 Convention in Denver, we heard numerous compliments about how the conference was one of the NBA's best.

Around 1980, Earle and I, along with three other friends, started a joint venture called Associated Capital Enterprises (ACE). The objective of the venture was to invest in real estate throughout the state of Colorado. At its peak, ACE owned between 12 and 15 properties, both in Denver and the Greater Colorado Springs areas. Earle was a key member of the venture in that he maintained books and records on ACE's investments and took the lead in ensuring that the group made appropriate arrangements to collect rents and pay all necessary obligations on behalf of ACE. As noted above with regard to the NBA Convention and its success, Earle, as it relates to his ACE participation, consistently demonstrated loyalty, foresight, sound business planning, and a collaborative approach to decision making. He was definitely a team player who helped to resolve relationship issues between venture members when they became frayed. Ultimately, ACE liquidated its holdings and ceased operations due to declines in the real estate industry.

One of Earle's lifelong strengths and interests has been his commitment to the African American experience and the importance of understanding our history and applying that history to racial issues in contemporary society. While Earle lived in Denver, our families met on a regular basis to watch the PBS award-winning documentary series "Eyes on the Prize." It chronicled the civil rights movement in the United States from 1954 to 1965. After watching each episode at one of our homes, there was an in-depth discussion of what we had watched and its implications for our people. Earle's comments were always insightful, thought-provoking, and on point.

I am proud of Earle Jones's numerous contributions to Denver, Colorado, and its citizens while he lived here from 1977 to 1994. Earle got involved in the life of this community in multifaceted ways that made a real difference. After he left Denver, many in the community commented positively about Earle's contributions and the fact that he was missed. It was special for Earle and Linda to return to Denver in 2006 to celebrate Sam Cary's 35th anniversary. Earle enjoyed the opportunity to reconnect with friends and fellow attorneys.

Wiley Y. Daniel
Senior U.S. District Judge
Denver, Colorado

EARLE JONES, MY COLLEAGUE & MY FRIEND

In life, God brings some special people in to your path that He allows you to work with or spend time with at social settings or in worship. Some of these individuals you know for a season, some for just a few months, and then there are those special souls that God simply connects you with for what seems a lifetime. Earle is one of those special souls for me.

Earle and I met many decades ago when he began working for Comcast in our Maryland, Delaware, and Washington, DC, Mid-Atlantic Division of the company. As I recall, Earle had a very unique position with Comcast. He was the only individual working for a regional operations group who oversaw our relationships with our federal elected officials. Being in the Washington, DC, market, it made perfect sense to have someone as capable as Earle with very good relationships keeping an eye on our federal affairs issues.

Since I was in the Eastern Region of Comcast, Earle and I would meet occasionally at events and government affairs meetings held throughout the years. We had some wonderful times at some beautiful venues around the country thanks to Sheila Willard and her amazing creativity when it came to planning fun events. As I got to know Earle personally, I discovered a gGodly man with a servant's heart, a humble man with little ego or need to be in the limelight. Earle was simply a hard worker who cared deeply about the job he did representing Comcast. A man of great integrity who you could trust and you knew that his word was his bond. If he told you something, you could "take it to the bank." You knew it was the truth, and that he would stand by his word.

After many years, Comcast merged our two operating divisions, and I experienced a new and professionally and personally rewarding role as Earle's boss and the senior vice president of the new Eastern Division. I wondered at the time if this would change our relationship. For some people, it is difficult to transition to a new role and reporting structure in a company, but not for Earle or for me. I found these years of having Earle as part of my senior leadership team to be some of the most exciting and joyful years in my business career. Earle was the consummate professional who knew what his job was, and he was determined to do it to the best of his abilities.

As often happens in companies as they grow, Earle and I experienced company reorganization, and Earle left my team to become part of the newly formed Federal Affairs Team working in Washington, DC.

While we did not see each other as often, nor communicate as regularly as we had, I knew that Earle always had my back, and I had his. When we did speak, there was always a sense of well-being and trust. Our friendship over so many years had grown to a point that I knew, without a shadow of a doubt, what so many of our members of Congress and senators knew . . . that Earle was a man of integrity, trustworthy, and loyal. Earle's leadership and the example he has set as part of our federal government Affairs Team has contributed to the success and remarkable results they have achieved.

I am thankful that Earle has been an important part of the amazing growth of Comcast for so many years; however, I am even more thankful that he has been my friend.

David Breidinger, Senior Vice President
Government Affairs
Comcast Northeast Division
(And Friend of Earle)

MY PERSONAL CHAMPION

I'm not sure when I first met Earle . . . We were both lobbyists in a crowded field. Earle and I really began working together during my time at Bryan Cave (Comcast was a client). We walked the halls together, attended fundraisers together, and counseled each other.

During my time at Bryan Cave, circumstances changed and I began entertaining the thought of starting my own lobbying firm. I shared this thought with Earle. I am 100 percent certain that my desire to "hang my own shingle" would not have happened had I not had support from Earle, my personal champion.

Earle will tell anyone I'm younger than most consultants he works with. I'm unmistakably a Louisiana girl—fiery, ready for battle, and eager for a win. Earle balances me. His words and presence brings calm, positive energy, and a useful perspective to any given situation. To be clear, Earle gives me the signal to do a little damage when warranted.

Working with Earle is never a chore. We can work on increasing his willingness to text and/or use e-mail, but we have time for that. No matter if we're meeting with a member of Congress, a staffer, or a colleague in a congressional office, the halls of Congress, or a fundraiser, Earle is Earle. He is always himself. He always speaks his truth. He always leads by example.

Earle has contributed to my personal and professional growth in so many ways; I simply cannot express them all. Over at least the last 6 years, I have experienced Earle selflessly give of himself—his time, his knowledge, and his "lessons learned."

So, someone else may read this and say, "Hey, Earle is my personal champion too." That may very well be the case . . . I'm willing to share. Besides, Earle wouldn't want any of us fighting over him . . . that's just not the man he is.

Jennifer M. Stewart, Ph.D., President
Stewart Strategies & Solutions, LLC

THE "COMCAST CARES" GIVER

Comcast believes in giving back to communities across the country. There are several ways Comcast gives back, but two ways in particular are through Comcast Cares Day (the annual, company-wide day of community service for employees) and by contributing through the United Way campaign.

Although I work with Earle on a daily basis as his assistant, the importance of community investment partnerships stands out the most to me.

Right before the beginning of April or mid-October of each year, you can count on Earle to do everything possible to get 100 percent participation from Comcast and NBCUniversal employees in the DC office.

From the initial e-mail informing us of the upcoming events to the personal office visits, Earle is working hard to get his colleagues involved with local community projects or blood drives. He encourages families to come along to help with painting murals, planting flowers and plants, mulching, building vegetable gardens, and general clean up. Earle's determination and dedication gives some of us the extra boost we need to sign up and volunteer for the various projects during Comcast Cares Day.

Then, October rolls around and Earle is coordinating the efforts for community involvement again. You can find him walking office to office letting everyone know that no amount is too small to pledge and making phone calls to make sure the United Way campaign is successful.

Not only does Earle give of his time, he genuinely cares about giving back to the community and getting everyone to rally together in support of Comcast Cares Day and United Way.

Eldean K. Penn, Administrative Assistant
Federal Government Affairs
Comcast Corporation

"EXECUTIVE" GIVING BACK

Upon our introduction, I remember thinking of the actor, James Earl Jones. It was in early 2000 when I was introduced to the head honcho of District Cablevision.

He was then promoted to the government affairs team at Corporate aka the federal team in Washington, DC. It was in this role that I really got to know Earle Jones. Earle would call me occasionally to assist with a customer escalation for one of the senators or congressmen that resided in Northern Virginia, and it took teamwork to get those issues resolved efficiently.

In early 2000, the company put together a company-wide day of caring called Comcast Cares Day. Earle was the first to participate and would put together his workplace team and down the line, worked on getting employees at NBC4 and NBCUniversal involved. He single-handedly contacted his colleagues, friends, family, and consultants and talked up Comcast Cares Day so that everyone would give back on this one day each year. I remember back in 2010, we cleaned, painted, mulched, and pulled out tree stumps at Spingarn High School. Out of the 500+employees that attended, Earle elected to dig up the tree stumps. It was hard work, but at the end of the day, we were all truly pleased at the end result. He is the hardest working "executive" that isn't afraid to get his hands dirty and dig in to make a difference in the communities where we live, work, and serve.

Earle is a man that does not compromise his integrity. He does what is right and just. He gives back to his community and paves the way for others to lead.

Veronica Santos-Mazzuchi
Colleague and Friend

A PERSONAL AND PROFESSIONAL STYLE TO IMITATE

Dear Earle,

When I met you during the first phase of the AT&T transaction in DC, it was "friendship at first sight". You were so wonderful to me: you taught me so much about local DC politics and cable operations. I couldn't have had a better trainer. You truly prepared me for the later larger AT&T transaction. You also were so supportive of my team: answering questions and needs without complaint.

Transactions and work aside, I always admired your personal and professional style. You always displayed such warmth for friends and colleagues. In the toughest moments -- even when you were faced with your own personal challenges -- you always had that smile and a hug. Your kindness was always contagious.

Thank you for having been so much a part of my Comcast life, As I exit the company for retirement, you are one of the people with whom I want to stay in contact. You are too special a friend to leave behind.

Thank you for everything Earle,

Sheila Willard

ONE OF MY "GREATEST"

I am a really sports minded person so I want to use a sports analogy to describe Earle. Have you ever played Kick the Can? If you don't know the game it is part hide and seek, part tag, part chase and sometimes used as a rite of passage. In my neighborhood it was a real sport. We played it in our whole neighborhood not just in the yard. You know that kind of neighborhood where the houses are not too far apart? Not many cars going up and down the street. There are a lot of kids to playing. They are all shapes and ages. You might not have been the smallest but there were some pretty big kids, older and faster than you.

The first time I played there was a kid who was in charge. He was big and fast. He made the teams, he set the boundaries and he told us the rules. He had a dominating, intimidating sort of personality. As a new player to the game he left me feeling lost and uncertain how to proceed. THAT IS NOT EARLE!

Earle is the kid on the block who has been around for a while. He does not typically seek to be the center of attention. In fact in some ways he was very quiet. He was the boy who helped the new kids learn how to win the game. He helped them get on a good team. Showed them were to hide in the neighborhood. He made sure that we did not run through the wrong yards and stayed away from the mean kids. He knew all the players strengths and weaknesses. He could always set a strategy that enabled his team to "kick the can." You wanted to be on his team because he would win. But you also always had a good time when you were on his team. That is how I see Earle.

I first remember meeting Earle when Comcast acquired AT&T in the district. Comcast had been chomping at the bit to get into the City. We were excited and it could be said a little arrogant about this opportunity. I remember when Earle first spoke. I heard that deep calm voice. He was short and to the point. He spoke with no flare, no dramatics, no grandiose promised. He was sure and steady. Over the years as I have worked with Earle I have come to really appreciate his style. He provides a great balance to me as a person who can be more of a ready, fire, aim personality. If you give him the chance he can help you really understand the business. Not just the P&L but the personalities that really drive the industry. He has kept me connected to great people in the organization. I count him as one my greatest.

Lelia True

THE STRENGTH OF EARLE JONES

"You never know how strong you are, until being strong is your only choice."
— Bob Marley

I am sure that many others contributing to this effort to honor Earle will talk of his accomplishments and proficiency as a government affairs professional. I was so honored when asked to write a few words about him, and I immediately thought of one trait that has always captured the essence of Earle – his strength. His physical strength, his strength of character, the strength of his skills on Capitol Hill, but most of all his strength in dealing with the numerous ordeals he has faced over the last decade or so.

I have had the pleasure of knowing and working with Earle since 2003, when I joined Comcast's government affairs team. I was instantly impressed with his knowledge of the business, his professional demeanor, and his ability to work with people. His co-workers, legislators, staff and others all hold Earle in the highest esteem.

As successful as Earle was in his career at Comcast, his greatest accomplishments were dealing with the personal struggles that would have shattered a weaker person. I watched Earle as he handled his father's passing, his wife's struggle with cancer and his own diagnosis with that terrible disease. Throughout all of these troubled times, Earle kept his grace, dignity and positive outlook. In fact, I think he would agree that he has become only stronger as he made it through these tests of character and faith.

Over the last decade or so, Comcast has grown significantly, and issues have become more complex and contentious. It would be easy for anyone in Earle's position to become completely absorbed in their work and lose perspective on what really matters. To Earle's credit, he remains the same humble, gracious and respectful individual as the day I met him 12 years ago.

So I thank Earle for his friendship, leadership, and service to the government affairs team. Most of all, I thank him for reminding us all of how strong we can be when we have to be.

Sean Looney

COMMON SENSE, INTERGRITY, AND HUMAN DIGNITY

When I started working at Comcast in 2005 my boss told me that the pace would be hectic, the landscape confusing, and that time at Comcast should really be measured in dog years! Those words were prophetic, but fortunately I have had the pleasure of working with Earle and he has done so much to help me navigate and understand this sometimes crazy world.

I can always rely on Earle to listen when I need help, to let me vent a little, and to help me arrive at a solution and feel good about the outcome. Earle never compromises the business, he has a keen understanding of how we are able to operate as a company, but he also factors in the policy and the politics. Most importantly, Earle adds common sense, integrity and human dignity to the equation. Earle's advice always leaves you able to look at yourself in the mirror and in the long term know you are doing what's best for the company and for your colleagues and yourself. I am so fortunate to have such a friend and mentor!

Rob Omberg

FRIENDS

Some of us may have slightly different definitions of what a friend means to us. But overall, I think we all agree that a friend is a person in our lives that we may always depend on, no matter what. Our friends are those who we trust fully and are able to ask for their advice whenever we need to.

Friendships are unique relationships because, unlike family relationships, we choose to enter into them. And unlike other voluntary bonds, like marriages and romantic relationships, they lack a formal structure. You wouldn't go months without speaking to or seeing your spouse or significant other (hopefully), but you might go that long without contacting a friend.

The voluntary nature of friendships makes it subject to life's whims in a way more formal relationships aren't. In adulthood, as we grow up and go away, friendships are the relationships most likely to take a hit. When we were younger, we would just call Johnny at a moment's notice and see if we could get together; now you may have to ask Johnny if he has a couple of hours to catch lunch in 2 weeks.

As we move through life, we make and keep friends in different ways. Some of us are independent; we make friends wherever we go and may have more friendly acquaintances than deep friendships. Others are a bit more discerning, meaning they have a few best friends they stay close with over the years, but the deep investment means that the loss of one of those friends would be devastating. The most flexible of us are the acquisitive—people who stay in touch with old friends, but continue to make new ones as they move through the world.

Earle's more of the acquisitive type—he still has friendships from middle and high school that he's in touch with on a frequent basis—they do an alumni breakfast twice a year; guys he played, watched, and went to sports events with; book discussions groups and travel clubs he has participated in; classmates he went to law school with; friends from the time he lived in Denver 20 years ago; church members we socialize with frequently over the past 15 years; as well as several new friends he recently met in the Beta Nu Boulé in Northern Virginia. In addition, he developed a huge network of friendships through the community and professional boards, associations, and foundations he served on over the past 30 years.

It never ceases to amaze me how Earle finds the time to nurture friendships. Of course, there are more ways than ever today that we can communicate with friends, and the social media "multiplexity" theory suggests that the more platforms on which friends communicate—texting, twitter, and e-mailing, sending each other funny Snap chats, videos, e-cards, and links on Facebook, LinkedIn, and seeing each other in person—the stronger their friendship is. Social media can make things a bit weird by keeping friends continually in your peripheral vision. If you never see your friends in person, you're not really sharing experiences so much as just keeping each other updated on your separate lives. It becomes a relationship based on storytelling rather than shared living—not bad though, just not the same.

Even though Earle uses social media, his preferred means of communicating with friends is either in person or by phone, which include Skype for relatives in France and Facetime where he can see the friend or family member. He does believe in nurturing his friendships and is ever so careful to return calls or e-mails as expeditiously as a possible. Earle will never have an unreturned call from friends.

FRIENDS ESSAYS

- **Maurita Coley-Flippin**, Vice President and Chief Operating Officer, Multicultural Media, Telecom and Internet Council

- **Mrs. Betty Gardner**, Owner, Gardner Realty

- **Mr. Winston Haythe, Esq.**, USA Retired Professor of Law and Attorney at Law

- **Mr. Ron Lewis**, Managing Director, WYNTER INDUSTRIES

- **Mr. Calvin Minor**, Retired Sales Executive, Xerox Corporation

- **Mrs. Veronica Minor**, Retired Principal, Fairfax County Public Schools

- **Mr. Edward Moawad, Esq.**, Managing Partner at Adams, Burton & Moawad P.

- **Mr. Rob Noch**, Senior Consultant, Booz Allen

- **Mrs. Diane Powers-Noch**, Director of Communications, Virginia Department of Health Professions

- **Mr. Robert Noch**, Education Specialist, John Tyler Community College

- **Mrs. Cateena L. Powers**, Senior Manager, COX Communications

- **Mr. David Powers**, Lieutenant Colonel, U.S. Air Force (Ret.)

- **Mr. James Simmons**, Master's Special Education, Special Education Teacher, Prince George's County Public Schools

- **Mrs. Mary Simmons**, Home Schooling of Daughters and Special Needs Foster Parenting

- **Mr. Dexter Williams**, Legislative Assistant, Holland & Knight LLP

- **Mr. Ricco Williams**, Retired, Federal Bureau of Prisons

A MAN FOR ALL SEASONS

While Sir Thomas More, a sixteenth-century chancellor in England, may have been lionized by British playwright Robert Bolt in his 1954 play titled *A Man For All Seasons*, that same catchy phrase can best describe another Renaissance man—albeit one born in the twentieth century—by the name of Earle F. Jones. Both More and Earle share a "creed," or a collection of virtues that range from artistry, to religion, to law.

I have the privilege of knowing Earle's lovely bride Linda Eatmon-Jones and working with her in a professional capacity on a board of directors some time before I was fortunate enough to meet him in a social context. I quickly learned that to know Earle is to love him—simply, no more and no less! He is the total embodiment of a well-educated, well-accomplished, and well-polished gentleman in the nation's capital. Yet, there is not a scintilla of conceit or arrogance in his entire being. Earle is truly a Great Guy in every possible way!

The occasion for initially getting to know Earle was one typically associated with anxiety for some, sheer chaos for others, and delicate moments that may border on disaster for more than a few: an American wedding. I met Earle when I was serving as the best man for the nuptials of a good friend. Earle, in his typically unassuming, quiet manner, was there to assist in every way possible, especially during those moments when lack of clarity and direction prevailed.

He was the epitome of unflappable grace under pressure with a clear head, as others in typical prewedding fashion tended to lose theirs! He was the voice of reason and calm, ready to do whatever had to be done to ensure that that moment when the presiding official declared, "I pronounce you man and wife!" arrived in what appeared to be a seamless, flawless instant that could be cherished by the happy couple and guests.

Only those who were truly conversant with all of the behind-the-scenes activities that went on—and indeed, that occur during almost any wedding—could truly appreciate the steady hand that Earle displayed. His voice of reason and his calm demeanor magically produced moments of tranquility that banished potential catastrophe just as much as a bright beam of light can banish darkness and gloom.

As a guest in Earle's and Linda's lovely home on any number of occasions, I have—not surprisingly—found him to be the consummate host. He has an uncanny way of eliciting the very best responses from his guests.

The nation's capital of Washington, DC, the United States of America, and the world at large, need more principled men such as Sir Thomas More and Earle F. Jones. Each has withstood the test of time; each is a man of utmost integrity; and each is a man for all seasons. The sixteenth century was blessed to have had Sir Thomas More. Equally as important, the twentieth and the twenty-first centuries are blessed to have Earle. Long may he live and prosper!

Colonel Winston McDonald Haythe, U.S. Army (Ret.)
Professor of Law and Attorney at Law

"SAVED, SURRENDERED, AND SERVING"

(Key Verse) Isaiah 6:8 . . . Then I heard the Lord say,
"Whom shall I send? Who will be our messenger?" I answered, "I will go! Send me."

As Christians, we are to live a life that is pleasing and according to God's will. The moment you accept the Lord as your Savior, that is where the journey begins. Once you have taken care of your need for salvation, you can begin your daily walk with God. Build a relationship with God through talking to Him in prayer and listening to Him through His Word; then you grow more and become more aware of Him leading your life. He will show you His will. We can't all be like Jesus. Our humanness and sin get in our way. But we can develop a teachable spirit. We can love God with our heart, soul, mind, and strength. We can let Him transform us into more selfless and more joyful people so that our character will reveal the likeness of Jesus.

My first encounter with Earle was in one of Antioch Baptist Church Men's Prayer Breakfasts. I often tried to recruit him to sing in the men's choir. He reminded me that singing was not his spiritual gift and reminded me that this quality doesn't come naturally to him. It is imparted by God through His Holy Spirit. After many attempts to persuade him to volunteer for a ministry and enlightening conversations regarding God, family, politics, careers, sports, etc., I was most impressed with his humble spirit, and within time, knew he will decide. It became quite clear to me that his desire was to learn and grow spiritually, volunteering for a ministry that he could share his spiritual gifts with, one that is committed to a true calling by God and demonstrates what is necessary to be a true servant.

Through various conversations and many meetings with him, it was quickly determined that Earl had that compelling desire to serve the Lord in some capacity. I could not deny that the Lord was using him, being accountable to God, family, church, and friends. Once he made up his mind to be a truly dedicated Christian, he was going to prepare himself to serve. During our monthly Prayer Breakfast, he would often participate, offering words of wisdom and demonstrating his willingness to be helpful and share his testimony about his love for God. I wanted to do something a little different so I asked Earle and Allen Sample to assist me in organizing an Auxiliary Committee to work on Outreach activities to expose the youth to internships, scholarships, and events that would enrich their spiritual growth and life choices. During his devotion and methodical thinking process, he decided this was God's intention to use his spiritual gifts to assess where he could be more useful for the work of God, often asking and faced with life-changing decisions, "Where to serve, what type of ministry, what training is required"? We worked countless hours, meeting monthly, Saturday mornings at the Marriott, Tyson Corner, to brainstorm, plan, and execute activities to support the initiatives of the church. It was through prayer, faith, and activities like this we developed a great friendship, enjoyed each other's families, and as believers in the redemptive work of Christ, his spiritual maturity elevated to new levels.

God wants us to be accountable to one another. What I learned from our relationship is that before one can ever lead the way God wants us to, we must learn to follow Him in all we do. Then, we can be effective as a leader in our home, our job, a leader who encourages our wife and children in their spiritual growth, and care for their emotional and physical needs. As my wife Veronica and I have enjoyed many social activities with his family and mutual friends, Christmas parties, weddings, tTheatre gGroup, and dDinners, we have admired his love and appreciation of being a family man and blessed by God. As he continues to grow, he uses his experiences to build lasting relationships with family and friends. Earle continues to keep his eyes on the goal, serving God, sharing his testimony, enlisting other Christians to be a part of the church ministry team, and witnessing to nonbelievers.

Through his unselfish ways, opening his home and heart to people he loves, I believe Earle knows there are two things we as Christians must do with the Gospel: one is to "believe it" and the second is to "live it." If we are not under God's authority, then we cannot be effective in authority. No one will want to follow a leader who is self-centered. After all, when we are self-centered, then we can't be God-centered.

Well, my good friend, we know how special you are. God has given you unique qualities, talents, and gifts. You are God's child created by Him. He loves you more than your earthly father, and He cares for you even when you feel worthless and far away. His love for you, His one-of-a-kind child, will never fail. It is not by accident we celebrate this day for you. Being as humble as you are, you will never boast, brag, or burden one to convince them why you think you are special. We congratulate you, and God validates it for you. **Psalm 139:16 says, "all the days are ordained for me."**

God bless you as you continue your journey and find steps, like Noah, who did not find favor because of his individual goodness, but because of his faith in God, to find favor in God's sight.

In HIS Love,
Friends in Christ, Calvin and Ronnie Minor

HALLMARKED AS OUR OLDER BROTHER

Each day we give thanks to God for inserting wonderful, influential, and kind people in our lives to share our walk and experiences in life. Earle is one of those chosen people; a blessing to all people he meets. He unselfishly extends his friendship and love of humanity for not only the few, but benefiting the many. For our family, Earle is cherished for being a lifelong friend and supportive leader, when life is both challenging and wonderful. Earle is hallmarked as our older brother.

Knowing Earle is appreciating a man who knows who he is and his family roots. Throughout our daily journey in military and business lives, working daylong shifts verses hours; traveling and returning thousands of miles around the globe; and persevering identity challenges and maturing faith, Earle remains rock-solid in his friendship and faith. Upon entering Earle's home, not only does his art and worldly collections reflect his connection with African American song and life, but, also the theme and pride of African beauty interwoven into the fabric of a complex world.

Earle was a great comfort to help Cateena in search of a new career path when the job environment was unfriendly and uncertain. Earle was a solid balance following the passing of our father, Lieutenant General Winston D. Powers, U.S. Air Force (Ret.).

Earle is a welcome face as he guides us to safe parking every Sunday at church, a place where we all share God's Word and warm embrace. As we arrive for annual Christmas parties and summer celebrations at his home, we feel the inclusion of his family and ours.

Earle is a consummate professional and inspiration to all people who appreciate hard work and knowing that each hand we hold is our chance to extend God's grace.

Thank you, Earle!!!
David and Cateena Powers

COOL, CALM, AND COLLECTED

It was just a normal occurrence, as after a business trip, both Earle and I would call each other to share our experiences and adventures. You see, Earle and I traveled extensively, sometimes together, and separately for the Fortune "5" corporations that we worked for. Earle would tell me about the tycoons he shared the corporate jet with and about the conversations they had, primarily about sports or the business at hand. I would share with "EJ" my discussions on our company planes and how difficult it was after a few drinks (on the plane) to stay away from topics like religion and politics. I truly enjoyed and valued our conversations as we would laugh together and sometimes agonize over how trying it was to hold on to each rung of the "corporate ladder."

But on this occasion, I was telling EJ about my trip to Indonesia and how I decided to take some vacation while there and visit the island of Bali. I remember explaining to him the peace and solitude I experienced at the Tanah Lot Temple. We talked about the beauty of the tropical waters and the calmness I felt sitting on the beaches and eating some of the most exotic and delicious fruits I had ever tasted. All the while, as I shared with EJ those surroundings, he seemed to be really engaged. I wrapped up my adventurous trip by telling EJ that out of all the places I had visited in the world, the sunsets in Bali, Indonesia, were simply spectacular. I told him it seemed I could just reach out and touch the sun. There was a long pause on the phone, and then EJ said, "I gotta go there." We ended our conversation and probably didn't speak for about 3 weeks.

One evening after watching an NBA game, I decided to call my buddy EJ and discuss the "horrible officiating" and "sloppy play," as we always did. But on this evening, it took an unusually longer time for EJ to answer. After so many rings, I decided to hang up and call back. This time, EJ answered, and I started off immediately by complaining about the game. EJ cut me off politely and said, "You know that breathtaking sunset you told me about in Bali?" I answered yes. EJ said in a calm and collected voice, *"I'm looking at it!!!"*

That's my friend EJ; still cool, calm, and collected; today, tomorrow, and beyond.

Ron Lewis
A Friend for Life

WISE COUNSELOR, MENTOR, AND FRIEND

From his loving marriage to Linda to stewardship of Stephen during his formative years and advances in his own successful high-profile career—it has been a joy and a pleasure for my husband, Bob Nock, and I to enjoy a more-than-15-year friendship with Earle Jones.

Along the way, Earle's greatest gift to us as a family has been his kind mentorship of our son Rob, now a businessman and consultant in his own right. Earle counseled Rob during his collegiate years just as he would a business associate, making himself available over dinners and through conversation to encourage Rob to chart a balanced work life plan. Today, I credit Earle's interest and wise counsel with being among the critical success factors that helped Rob Nock become the young man he is today. For that, we will be forever grateful.

Rob's parents, Diane Powers-Nock and Robert L. Nock

THE MENTEE MENTORS

Earle, I thank you for being a wonderful mentor and friend. I'm not sure if you're aware, but your influence contributed to my decision to pursue a career in consulting at Booz Allen. Along the way, I followed your lead and mentored a young man in need of a role model through Big Brothers Big Sisters (BBBS).

Over lunches and before playing video games, we worked hard to improve his math grades and self-confidence. He is now on a path to college. Through your mentorship, I've learned so much—especially how rewarding it can be to support the growth and development of the next generation.

As a young man, I was so impressed that you were such a dedicated and faithful family man. You are a student of life, always willing to share your knowledge and wisdom. Your diverse knowledge in all subject matters from politics, religion, education, finance, community service, sports, world affairs, entertainment, etc., is the gift that keeps on giving.

Rob Noch

A RIGHTEOUS BROTHER

I got to know Earle probably in the late 1990s, in the fast-paced world of cable television. My law firm represented Comcast, so he was a client, and as longtime professionals in the media and cable television industries, we had a shared goal of increasing minority ownership and employment in the industries. He is also a longtime board advisor of my nonprofit, Multicultural Media, Telecom, and Internet Council (MMTC), as well as NAMIC (the National Association of Multi-Ethnicity in Communications), often serving quietly behind the scenes like an Olivia Pope, and leveraging his corporate experiences and connections to help solve problems within both organizations.

Over the years, my husband, Paul, and I developed a deep interest in learning the untold stories of our African history. When we started attending the monthly IKG Cultural Circle lectures conducted by Tony Browder at the IKG Cultural Center, I wasn't surprised to find Earle there. The lectures and Egypt in the Potomac Tours were held primarily at the historic Anthony Bowen YMCA, now the Thurgood Marshall Trust off U Street in Washington, DC, a sacred place where men of African descent such as Langston Hughes stayed since they were not allowed to sleep in the "other" YMCA, or even in most of the hotels in the District of Columbia. As with most things, Earle was way ahead of the game; Earle had already journeyed with Tony to Egypt (Kemet) to tour the historic pyramids and other sites, and to study the history of Egypt when it was inhabited by the indigenous black people of the Nile Valley.

When our offices were only a block from each other, Earle and I would grab an afternoon coffee, partially to decompress, partially to mull over how best to solve the problems that impacted black people on the planet. Getting to know Earle as a person apart from Earle the client was a true honor; his mind and spirit are so far ahead of the rest of us mortals, and his knowledge of his history and commitment to his people are laudable, and rare.

I was so honored to have been contacted by Linda to contribute to this keepsake for Earle. My husband Paul calls Earle a "righteous brother," which is the ultimate compliment from one brother to another, so this will be a tribute from the two of us. Earle is a wonderful professional and a dedicated colleague and friend, but there is one thing I know for sure: Earle is so deserving of such a phenomenal woman as Linda, whom I don't yet know as well as I know Earle, but I know enough to know that he has chosen well.

Congratulations, my dear friend. May God **CONTINUE** to chase you down with blessings of every kind!

Maurita Coley Flippin, Esq., and Paul Flippin (friends from Cole Raywid & Braverman, Davis Wright Tremaine, MMTC, and IKG)

IMPRESSIONS OF EARLE

We have come to know Earle in the last several years. Earle is the father-in-law of the oldest of our five daughters, Heather Eatmon. Earle works very hard, but when he can, he fully participates in many family activities . . . birthday fun, barbecues, and our holiday get-togethers. He has been totally supportive of Heather and Steve and their children, Ryan and Rachael . . . and his sister Sylvia and all his loved ones in France.

He is a loving and loved: husband; father; father-in-law; grandfather; brother; uncle; great-uncle; and friend!

The first phrase that comes to mind when we think of Earle is unfailing kindness. He cares. He is concerned. He is interested. You get the feeling he is looking beyond his own best interests for the interests of others in his life. (Philippians 2:4, "Let each of you look not only to his own interests, but also to the interests of others.")

Our impression is one of trust, that I know he wants to uplift the loved ones and friends in his life. He does not have a hidden agenda to use others; but instead, wants to bless others . . . This is why he is a person who can be trusted. He is humble. He is honest. He reminds me of Nathanael, who Jesus said, "Behold an Israelite in whom there is no guile." In short, he is a wonderful man whom we are honored to know!

Mr. and Mrs. (Mary) James Simmons

FAMILY FRIEND BECOMES A MENTOR

I've known Earle since I was about 10 years old (maybe even younger). I was at his house one day, about 15 years ago, for one of the Jones's famous cookouts. At this cookout, he said something to me that resonated, and I don't think he knew the impact he left on a young, impressionable teenager.

So, it was about 15 years ago where Linda and Earle had a cookout at their home. My dad and I arrived at the house midevening. The usual suspects were at the cookout, which included family, friends, and the occasional person I had never seen before. Everyone was friendly and the conversation was good (at least the parts I could understand as a young teen).

Eventually, the midevening turned into night. There were a couple of us sitting at the kitchen table talking about something. I don't recall exactly what we were talking about. But what I do remember is that for at least 5 minutes or so, I was the focus of the conversation as I was answering questions. I noticed that Earle had this look on his face as I was answering these questions. I couldn't figure out what the issue was. So, naturally, as a teen, I had moved on and forgotten about it in a span of a few minutes.

As time passed, everyone played their role in cleaning up or leaving quickly so they wouldn't have to clean up. Just as my dad and I were leaving, Earle pulled me aside. In fact, he pulled me outside. I could tell this was about to be a teachable moment. Why else would Earle take me outside where no one could hear the conversation?

He wanted to bring something to my attention. He told me that my pronunciation of the word "ask" was wrong. I pronounced it as "ax" instead of "ask." Earle told me that "you have to be careful about how you speak because people make judgments, and while it may not be fair, it is a reality."

I appreciated that moment, and it meant a lot to me because it told me that someone took the time to correct me when they didn't have to say anything at all. At that moment, our family friend became my mentor and biggest supporter in my education and professional career.

Earle is a great man who has inspired me to be great. As a young adult, he constantly encourages me and challenges my political and life views. He cares very deeply about people, the community, and he's one of my greatest champions all the time.

Mr. Dexter Williams

AN AWESOME LANDLORD & FRIEND

In 2005, Earle's father reached the point where he could not managed his home and required 24-hour assistance. Earle and his sister decided to move their father to a care facility so he could get the best support needed. This was a very difficult decision for both because their family home had over 50 years of memories for the family, but more importantly, it had the life story of their father's career. And what a career that was. He had a lab in the basement because he was a distinguished scientist, and so many pictures because he loved taking pictures. Artwork, awards, trophies, newspaper articles of his community work, books galore, etc., were all there.

Neither Earle nor his sister wanted the house to sit empty, and they were not prepared to sell it. At that time, I was moving from Maryland to DC and was looking for a place to rent. I had known Earle through Linda for about 4 years and really admired him from a distance, plus he took time to serve as a positive role model for my son Dexter during those years. I'm not sure how the conversation came up, but as always, Earle was the thorough and caring person—it was like I was talking to a family member and not a new landlord.

I do not have enough words to describe how much I appreciate and thank Earle for giving me a chance to "care" for his family heirlooms. I knew how much they meant to each of them. I was a pallbearer at his father's funeral, and it was like I knew his life's story from the many wonderful things in the house. Over the years, his sister, niece, Linda, and Earle, have gone through many things and removed them from the property, but it was never an issue with them being there. Earle is such a decent man that always does right by people—you just want to do right by him.

I cannot say enough about the "landlord" part of him—he's awesome—he anticipates the need for things, and they are taken care of before they become problems. He's so respectful of my feelings and privacy; he shows care and concern for my son, my mother, and brother as well. I will always work to keep the Jones's home the best-looking one on the street. I do that to honor the great man God put in my path during my hour of need.

Earle is an amazing man of God, loves his family, is committed to his friends, and I am fortunate to know him.

Mr. Ricco Williams

LOYAL FAMILY MAN AND FRIEND

Earle is my best friend's husband, and I have known him for years. If there was anyone out there that is perfect for my friend Linda, it would be Earle. Earle is a great family man who is loyal, caring, hardworking, and a true gentleman.

He is a great role model for all the men out there. Our families used to get together for dinners, parties, and celebrations. One of the most memorable times was when we all gathered to play Gestures. Gestures is a game where you have to act out ridiculous things, and Earle was a great sport and played along! He was able to let his guard down and have fun with us all. Earle is not only a great professional, but also a wonderful friend who is able to partake in the wildest events to make us all laugh.

Your Dear Friends,

Ms. Liana Lekprichakul
Mr. & Mrs. (Andrea) Brooks Randolph

PARTY HOST EXTRAORDINAIRE

If someone asked me to describe Earle Jones, I would not hesitate! I know him as a loyal, supportive husband to my dear friend Linda, and I know him as a party host extraordinaire! Earle is such a wonderful host. He is so attentive to each and every guest, and they do have many guests at their Christmas parties. Earle has this way of making everyone feel as if they each have his undivided attention. He's charming, gracious, and just plain fun to be around!

I wish you continued blessings, my friend.

Ms. Betty Gardner

NOT JUST ANY MAN

Earle is a true man! One of a kind! Trustworthy; a man of his word! Open a dictionary and look under "Great Man" and you'll see his picture! He's charming, handsome, and well-dressed. His humility prevents him from stating the obvious, and I wonder if he sees himself in this light. If there is anyone I would want to be in a bunker with in hard times, it would be Earle—he is that rare friend you can depend on. A thought, both comforting and frightening at the same time! He is a rarity; of a generation long gone; comforting that we are privileged to have him in our lives! Frightening is the same thought! Where do we find an Earle?

Let's celebrate him! For when he's gone, God willing, in a very, very long time, we will surely miss him as he will leave a void that cannot be filled by just any man.

To the Best!!!
Mr. Edward Moawad, Esq.

BOARDS,
ASSOCIATIONS &
FOUNDATIONS

Life's most persistent and urgent question is, "What are you doing for others?"
—Martin Luther King Jr.

A board or foundation of directors is a body of elected or appointed members who jointly oversee the activities of a company or organization. They typically are volunteer positions working to implement a vision and mission of an organization and to sustain its operations. Boards promote the social, economic, educational, and cultural welfare of communities and individuals. Serving as a nonprofit board member is one of the most challenging and rewarding of volunteer assignments. While appointment or election to a board or foundation is an honor, board members have important legal and fiduciary responsibilities that require a commitment of time, skill, and resources. Boards select on two basics: capabilities and character.

Throughout his career, Earle's capabilities, character, and passion to serve others stood out, and he was sought by various organizations to serve as a board member. He has served as officers of many boards over the years. Below is a highlight of several of the boards, associations, and foundations Earle served on over the past 35 years. His involvement in each has contributed to significant accomplishments impacting the lives of thousands of minorities. There are also a host of committees, panels, and workshops Earle has shared his knowledge and skills on, dating back to law school, his days in Denver, and the cable and communications industry.

National Association for Multi-Ethnicity in Communications (NAMIC) New York, NY—Its mission is to educate, advocate, and empower multiethnic diversity in the communications industry. NAMIC has over 35 years of diversity, leadership, and empowerment experiences. Earle served on the NAMIC board of directors with about 25–30 executives and leaders in the cable communications industry. He served on the board for approximately 17 years, starting in the early '90s. Earle served as the treasurer to the board and on various committees, including the Urban Markets Conference (later it became the national NAMIC Conference), Finance, and Development. Earle played a role in helping to organize regional NAMIC meetings which focused on the operations side of the business. He also served on the annual breakfast committee several times and was very instrumental in restructuring the by-laws, allowing it to become the dynamic organization it is today. Earle was a mentor for several years to the DC chapter of NAMIC.

The Greater Washington Urban League (GWUL) is a major interracial, nonpartisan, nonprofit social services and civil rights organization with headquarters in DC and offices in the District and Prince George's County, Maryland. The mission is "to increase the economic and political empowerment of minorities and to help all Americans share equally in the responsibilities and rewards of full citizenship." The approaches of social work, advocacy, law, and other disciplines are used to empower communities. Earle served on the board of directors from 1999–2012, representing Comcast. As a board member, he held several executive board positions: first vice president, secretary, and treasurer, and also led a host of program and fundraising committees, especially the acquisition of the new building in DC that houses all operations.

The Congressional Black Caucus Foundation (CBCF) is an American educational foundation. It conducts research on issues affecting African Americans, publishes a yearly report on key legislation, and sponsors issue forums, leadership seminars, and scholarships. Although linked with the Congressional Black Caucus (CBC), the Congressional Black Caucus Foundation is a separate nonprofit group that runs programs in education, health care, and economic development. The CBCF board of directors is comprised of members of the U.S. Congress, business executives, and leaders in government and in the nonprofit sectors. Board members generously volunteer their time, expertise, and resources to support the CBCF's mission. Led by R. Donahue Peebles, as chair, the board of directors' guidance is vital to the growth and success of CBCF's programs and initiatives. Earle serves as the current secretary to the executive board of directors.

The Congressional Black Caucus Institute (CBCI), incorporated in 2000, is a nonprofit, nonpartisan, social purpose organization playing a pivotal role in training the next generation of political leaders and providing voters with relevant information regarding issues in their communities.

The CBC Institute's premier policy conference is held in Tunica, Mississippi, annually, and is representative of the CBC Institute's ongoing commitment to meeting its overall mission—educating today's voters and training tomorrow's leaders. The policy sessions and luncheons provide a perfect opportunity for a cross-section of committed individuals, including: community leaders, state, and locally elected officials, private sector leaders, labor leaders, academics, and government officials to join in discussions with members of Congress and highly qualified issue-specific experts.

Earle has been a member of the CBCI for several years, attending the policy institutes as well as having Comcast host a policy conference at Comcast NBCUniversal Studios in Florida in 2015.

Covenant House Washington in Washington, DC, is an affiliate of Covenant House International, the nation's largest privately funded nonprofit organization responding to the needs of young people who suffer from homelessness, abuse, and neglect. Covenant House Washington's mission is to serve suffering children of the street with absolute respect and unconditional love. Earle served on the board of directors from 2003–2010. Vincent Gray, former mayor of DC, was board chair during Earle's board tenure. Earle served in several board officer positions, as well a very generous fundraiser.

Smart Activities for Fitness and Education (SAFE) DC was established in 1993 by Carroll "Spyke" Henry. As a lifelong resident of the District of Columbia, Mr. Henry recognized the need to provide youth with supervised, productive, and engaging activities. The absence of quality and affordable tennis programs for inner-city DC youth led to the founding of SAFE. Through the implementation of organized athletic and mentoring activities, SAFE has positively impacted the lives of hundreds of youth in the District in building their character and self-esteem and improves their academic performance. Earle has served as the chairman of the SAFE board since 2011.

The Faith & Politics Institute was founded in 1991 and has served hundreds of members of Congress and congressional staff by offering experiential pilgrimages, reflection groups, retreats, and public forums. In a world that is increasingly interconnected, they do this work with Congress because of their ties to a broad constituency and their leadership in local, national, and global policy.

The institute does more than create safe spaces for dialogue; it takes strategic steps to promote leadership that will have a positive impact on the tone and effectiveness of Congress, and through the Congress, the nation.

As the Comcast representative, Earle has participated in several pilgrimages, retreats, and public forums.

Most notably, he participated in the 50th Anniversary of "Bloody Sunday" with its annual Congressional Pilgrimage to Alabama in 2015. The institute brought together an unprecedented number of senators and members of Congress in a bipartisan fashion to honor the civil rights struggle of the past.

Beta Nu Boulé was established as a member Boulé in Northern Virginia in 1978. On November 15, 1981, a charter was issued approving new members of Beta Nu Boulé. Nearly 4 decades later, Beta Nu has a very large membership of distinguished Archons forging a rich history by the significant achievements and contributions of its Archons.

In 1986, the Beta Nu Education Foundation was established to promote the advancement of male African American high school students in Northern Virginia. Since 2007, Beta Nu Boulé, through its education foundation, has awarded more than $150,000 in scholarships to academically superior students as well as to those who make an honest effort and deserve a chance. Beta Nu believes education is key to future success. In 2015, Earle was inducted as an Archon of Beta Nu Boulé.

BOARDS ESSAYS

- **Ms. Maudine Cooper**, Past President & CEO, Greater Washington Urban League

- **Mr. Carroll "Spyke" Henry**, Founder and Executive Director, SAFE

- **Mr. Joseph Lawson**, Content & Acquisition Verizon/go90

- **Mr. Jerry Moore III**, (Former) Chairman of the Board, Greater Washington Urban League

- **Ms. Loretta Polk, Esq.** Vice President & Associate General Counsel, National Cable & Telecommunications Association

- **Ms. Wanda Townsend**, Vice President Government Relations, National Cable & Telecommunications Association

9/11/2001—THE DAY THE WORLD TRADE TOWERS WENT DOWN

I always enjoyed talking to Earle. He was one of the few people that I can say that virtually, every time I spoke with him, I learned something. I was just finishing 2 years as NAMIC president. Earle had been one of my nearest and most trusted advisors on the board.

We were at the opening of the 2001 NAMIC Conference in Times Square at the Millennium Hotel. It was a little after 9:00 a.m. when the conference opened. I went out in the hallway to speak with a friend who was visibly shaken up, who told me to look at the TV monitor. A plane had crashed into the World Trade Center.

After the second plane hit, it was very clear that this was a terrorist attack. It was also clear that there might be more. We were in Times Square, one of the most-known symbols of America and American culture, so there was a possibility that there might be another attack in our vicinity.

Earle had been a person that everyone could count on to get great advice. Earle, the NAMIC executive director, the new president who was succeeding me, and a few other folks, and I gathered together to discuss something we previously would have thought was unthinkable—closing the NAMIC national conference with people from all over the country less than an hour after it started.

We decided to shut down the conference with Earle chipping in his usual wise and sage like advice. We made the announcement to a stunned crowd. People rushed to exit doors, many going to the TV sets, and stood there hypnotized, some shaking their heads, others slowly mumbling soliloquies of disbelief, while others rushed to their rooms to pack so they could leave town. One woman sprinted out of the building into Times Square when she realized that her cousin worked at the World Trade Center.

Earle and I began to ponder what this meant, and then it hit both of us. Earle said that if there was another attack in Times Square, we at least needed face masks or something to filter out the poison and smoke. We hurriedly walked to the closest drugstore and both bought a small box of masks each. Then we walked back to the conference hotel, which had, by then, mostly emptied out.

Times Square was not attacked that day. But now I work in the Times Square area. Each day as I pass by that drugstore (even though it was 15 years ago), I always relive that moment, for a moment. *I scold myself for not letting go of it, but I cannot.*

It was a time of real mortal fear and terror in my life, and I am glad that my friend Earle was there with me.

Joe Lawson
Content & Acquisition
Verizon/go90

Feeds the hungry . . . Tends to the sick . . . Houses the homeless . . . Aids the helpless . . . And cheers the hopeless.

These are all the answers. The question is: what does the Greater Washington Urban League do for our community?

Washington, DC, is a beautiful city. But it hasn't become one on its own actions. Indeed, many of us have contributed, and beauty has been the collective end of our labor. For that we can congratulate ourselves. But, as in most things, there are those among us that excel in charity and achievement. And it is for this reason that one's attention quickly falls to Earle Jones.

Earle was a significant contributor to the beauty of our city *before* he came to the Greater Washington Urban League. Indeed, it was because he became known to us as such that we pursued and prevailed upon him to join our board of directors. Membership on our board did not diminish his energy or his dedication to enhancing the social fabric of our city. Earle was always there when needed: whether it be for moral, physical, or financial support. Earle always found the will and the time to provide assistance to us as we carried out those missions that were important to us.

Earle Jones, your dedication and steady contributions to our Greater Washington Urban League have been extraordinary, even when compared to those of a board of directors populated by high achievers. You are appreciated and will not go unrecognized.

And so, I congratulate and thank you for all that you have done to enhance the beauty, spirit, and brotherhood of our city.

A good way to judge a man is to evaluate what he does for those who he knows can bring him no material benefit.

JERRY A. MOORE, III
(Former) Chairman of the Board
GREATER WASHINGTON URBAN LEAGUE INC.

A MODERN-DAY "ATLAS"

In Greek mythology, Atlas is the Titan god sentenced by the Olympian god Zeus to hold the world up on his shoulders forever. There have been many times during his illustrious career as a corporate cable executive when Earle, alone, with only temporary assistance from me (his Heracles), has shouldered the burden of championing and defending the cable industry before the Congressional Black Caucus (CBC).

I have known Earle for 20-plus years. We have worked together on many issues, participated on many congressional panels, and even shared some downtime on business trips. It is difficult for me to single out any one specific situation or experience that illustrates why I believe he is a modern-day Atlas; however, since memories tend to fade when you get older, I will stick to the most recent one.

In this highly competitive video marketplace, the cable industry is constantly under attack by competitors who try to gain an unfair advantage through regulation in order to disrupt or upend our business models while remaining regulatory-free themselves. This is particularly true of many well-heeled companies in the tech community. Recently, during the Thanksgiving holiday, Earle and I were called upon to garner support from CBC members to prevent the tech community from disaggregating our video content through an FCC-imposed mandate. I will not bore you with the details, but let it suffice that this was a most daunting task to even get the members to understand such a complex and technical issue.

Contrary to urban legend, Earle's company is not the only video company serving every home in America. Far from it. Earle, on the other hand, is universally respected by CBC members, including those who represent districts outside his company's service areas. With few exceptions, Earle is the face of the cable industry for most CBC members.

So, on this occasion, I turned to Earle to help educate CBC members and their staff about this issue. He rallied to the challenge. Over the course of 2 weeks, Earle was part of the telecom coalition who met with CBC members and staff. It was Earle's persuasive arguments and perspectives that helped drive home how consumers, minority programmers, and the cable industry would be harmed by the tech proposal. When Congress recessed for Thanksgiving, Earle's advocacy continued.

Although family always comes first with Earle, he never refused to take my long-distance calls over the holidays to strategize about how to convey CBC member support for our position. We spent endless hours drafting language and e-mailing our champions on the Hill to bolster them. Even while our families patiently waited to sit down for Thanksgiving dinner, Earle and I were thinking of ways to pull off a successful campaign.

I admit I was a tad pessimistic about our chances for success, but Earle was the paradigm of optimism. He was right. Our efforts paid off royally when 30 members of the CBC signed a letter asking the FCC to refrain from doing what the tech community was seeking.

Unfairly, most of the accolades for our success were heaped upon me as the project manager. People in the industry tended to overlook the invaluable contributions Earle made. His were the shoulders I relied upon to make things happen. Earle was my sounding board, my counselor, my cheering squad, and my "go-to" guy. He never failed to produce or to give me a gentle nudge in the right direction. Even while others were praising me, Earle never begrudged the attention I received.

Earle is truly one of the unsung heroes of the cable industry. Members of Congress respect him. They value his wise counsel and his ability to distill complex issues into easily comprehended plain English. Other lobbyists, like myself, admire and look up to him. I am glad to be able to publicly give him the recognition he deserves. There is no better person whose shoulders I would trust to hold up the cable industry than Earle's—a modern-day Atlas.

Wanda Townsend
Vice President
Government Relations
National Cable Television Association

CHAIRMAN OF THE BOARD

Smart Activities for Fitness and Education (SAFE) is a nonprofit 501(c)3 organization that uses tennis programs to provide opportunities for youth in the District of Columbia to build their character and self-esteem and improve their academic performance. Through comprehensive tennis and educational programs and cultural enrichment activities, SAFE encourages youth to make better choices and teaches them to become confident, responsible, and valuable members of their community.

As the founder of SAFE in 1993 and having served as executive director, I knew we needed to have a board chairman with strong leadership, governance, and oversight skills for the organization to continue to serve the youth in the community.

When Earle agreed to join our board and accept the position as board chairman, I can truly say that he is the engine that keeps us going. Since his tenure as board chairman, we now have several lawyers, scientists (CDC), retired Dept. of Justice CPO, public relations manager, and a marketing/media guru. Because of Earle's fundraising skills, SAFE's bank account has grown.

As chairman, Earle has:

established partnerships with: Safeway, Coca-Cola, DC Department of Parks & Recreation, DC Public Schools, Department of Youth Rehabilitation Services, and DC Metropolitan Police Department

secured and managed public and private and corporate funding

assisted over 60 youth enter postsecondary education and secured over $1,053,540 in college scholarship funds and an additional $77,000 in private funds

developed and managed marketing and public relations collateral materials, including a Web site, brochures, flyers, invitations, general organizational information, and event-specific publications

defined strategies for and executes fundraising activities, program development, and community outreach

helped establish, recruit, and manage SAFE's Winter Tennis Program for kids ages 6–14 that has grown from six kids in 2010—presently 23 kids in 2016; they attend College Park Tennis Center every year from Nov.–March for "World Class" Training.

CARROLL "SPYKE" HENRY
Founder and Executive Director

VOICE OF CALM AND REASON

Earle and I served on the board of directors of NAMIC (National Association for Multi-Ethnicity in Communications) for over 18 years. When we joined the board, the cable industry was still relatively young and making its mark building out service in new communities and launching new programming channels. These were the days before the Internet, social media, TV on-demand, DVRs, and big-ticket original cable programming like *Game of Thrones* and *Mad Men*. Cable was rapidly changing the television landscape with an array of new channels and experiencing the economic, regulatory, and social growing pains of any new disruptive medium of communications. During our almost 2-decade tenure on the board, we saw the industry mature and shared many great experiences with our NAMIC colleagues.

Earle and I met in 1989 or 1990 when he moved back to Washington from Denver, Colorado, where he had been working for TCI, then the largest cable company in America. He joined the TCI Washington office to work on cable policy and regulatory matters. I had recently joined the National Cable & Telecommunications Association (NCTA) in the Legal Department, also responsible for handling communications policy and regulatory work before the FCC and other agencies. We hit it off immediately, partly because we were both native Washingtonians, but mainly because we had similar interests, backgrounds, and worked well together. We just connected—a DC thing that's hard to explain. And then, of course, being among the few minorities working the policy front in this field, we shared information and looked out for each other.

Earle and I joined the board of NAMIC in the early '90s and worked together on a variety of committees, including the annual Urban Markets conference, the fundraising and finance committee, and the annual breakfast honoring outstanding people of color at the cable industry's annual convention. The board was comprised of executives from the programming, operations, marketing, technology, and human resources fields. Earle and I were typically the only lawyers with a focus on government relations, so we were a little out of the box. But we enjoyed the opportunity to work on issues of importance to minorities in our industry and to provide the DC policy perspective. And we had fun too mixing it up with some talented cable folks at some great events in some great locations—New York, Los Angeles, Chicago, Palm Springs, Miami, even the Sonoma wine country. Those were the days . . .

Our meetings sometimes got into some controversial issues or proposals that seemed unrealistic or infeasible given our mission and budget. Earle was always a voice of calm and reason in the midst of the debate. He'd often wait until everyone got it out of their system and then weigh in with some rational comments and bring the temperature down in the room. Earle exuded common sense and a caring nature, so how could anyone not appreciate his input. Later, we'd share a laugh or express frustration about the meeting, but it was always for the good of the organization. Over time, we became the "elder statesmen" of the board as younger and more eager folks joined. New blood with fresh ideas is important for any organization to grow and thrive, and after almost 2 decades, it was time for Earle and me to quietly step down from the board. It was a great ride with my buddy Earle. I miss seeing him on a regular basis, but the connection, the DC connection, is always there.

Loretta Polk, Vice President & Assoc. General Counsel
National Cable & Telecommunications Association (NCTA)

A GENUINE NICE GUY

No matter how old you are or how long you've lived, there will always be a few people that you find memorable. Earle Jones is one of those people in my life.

I met Earle when I was still president of the Greater Washington Urban League (GWUL). Apparently, Earle had indicated to the National Urban League president that he wanted to work more closely with the League's local chapter.

That was the beginning of a great relationship, both personal and professional. Earle served many years on the GWUL board of directors; also, several times in an officer role, first vice chair, and second vice chair.

Earle took our mission: "to increase the economic and political empowerment of blacks and other minorities and to help all Americans share equally in the responsibilities and rewards of full citizenship" to heart and helped to encourage sponsorship from his company, Comcast. As a result, Comcast was very active and involved in all GWUL events and activities.

While a member of the board of directors, GWUL purchased a new building to house our growing organization and expanded services. This was a gigantic undertaking for the board. Earle's stewardship and commitment rose to the occasion. He never failed to deliver on his sponsorships. He was a very reliable and trusted board member of impeccable integrity. Earle continues to be a member of GWUL in support of our gala each year.

To say that someone is a nice guy may sound trite; however, Earle is a hardworking NICE guy.

Earle, stay committed to your principles and be strong.

Maudine R. Cooper, Past President and CEO
Greater Washington Urban League

CONGRESSIONAL
LOBBYING

GOVERNMENT AFFAIRS & CONGRESSIONAL LOBBYING

Writing about any aspect of Congress during an election year can be a bit dicey with all the campaign rhetoric going around 24/7. However, Earle has worked with congressional chiefs of staff (COS), legislative aides, and assistants for many years to ensure they can properly prepare their congressman on policies and proposed legislative issues affecting the cable industry. Earle has worked directly with the congressmen on many occasions.

This is another slice of the pie I get to see that many may not. Earle never compromises his integrity for the benefit of others. That's one of the reasons many on the Hill hold him in such high regard. He has seen the changing of the guard on the Hill many times over the years and has been able to establish new relationships as well as retain existing ones.

Earle is requested to travel frequently to their local or district fundraising benefits, issue-related speaker forums, and educational panels. As a cable industry expert and advocate, he is able to provide the educational perspective on an issue or policy. Since he grew up on the operations' side of the cable business as a general manager, he understands the policy and operations on behalf of ComcastNBCUniversal and TCI when he represented TCI.

People often ask him what his role is as a government affairs or government relations lobbyist. The short answer is that it is an educational process mixed in with a moderate amount of advocacy. Simply put, it is an essential component of any business that is subject to government regulations.

At its core, government affairs/relations is an educational process: educating business and industry leaders about the governmental process; educating government officials about the issues important to business or other constituencies; and educating governmental and business leaders, and the public about the potential consequences of legislation. Ultimately, what government affairs professionals do is make the case for their business or industry in the public policy arena. This is where Earle's passion for knowledge acquisition and traveling is a benefit.

In 2002, after Comcast acquired AT&T Broadband, Comcast moved into a leadership role in representing the cable industry's interests and the Comcast's interests in Washington, DC, as its footprint expanded from a minority of the Congress to covering most of the Congress. Earle was asked to transition from a field-based government affairs role in Comcast to join the growing Washington office and to take the lead in developing relationships with all of the diversity caucuses, including the Congressional Black Congress (CBC) and lobby on behalf of both cable industry's and company's interests. Earle continues to perform that role today and has earned a highly regarded relationship with the CBC and its foundation and institute. He currently serves as secretary of the CBC Foundation.

A great example of what a solid relationship between government and business can do regarding public policy and legislative regulations is the Comcast/General Electric acquisition of NBC Universal. Earle was a member of the Comcast Federal Affairs Legislative team that successfully obtained the Comcast/General Electric acquisition of NBCUniversal Federal regulatory approval in January 2011. Earle worked tirelessly to educate his assigned congressional members on the benefits of the acquisition to their constituents and districts.

CONGRESSIONAL ESSAYS

- **Congressman G. K. Butterfield**, North Carolina's 1st district

- **Congressman Gerry Connolly**, Virginia's 11th district

- **Congressman James Clyburn**, South Carolina's 6th district

- **Congressman Alcee Hastings**, Florida's 20th district

REFLECTIONS ON EARLE JONES
By Congressman Gerry Connolly (Virginia's 11th district)

I have known Earle Jones since before being elected to Congress, primarily though his wife, Linda. During my tenure on the Fairfax County Board of Supervisors, she was executive director of both the Fairfax Partnership for Youth and later the regional suicide prevention hotline CrisisLink, so I met them both through their commitment and passion to improving our community.

Although Comcast has a small footprint in Fairfax, primarily in Reston, which I was pleased to represent for 5 years as chairman of the board of supervisors, the company operates throughout Prince William, which I am now proud to represent in Congress. Earle, as a key player on the Comcast federal government relations team, has been an invaluable resource to me and my staff in addressing issues brought to us by our constituents, Comcast's customers. He also has been generous with his time and expertise in providing insight and discussing telecommunications matters that have come before Congress.

While some might accuse Earle of favoring his local congressman, he is known throughout the halls of Congress as an affable and effective emissary of Comcast and the telecommunications industry in which he has worked for the past 25 years. He was part of the legislative affairs team that helped educate members of Congress and obtain federal regulatory approval for Comcast's acquisition of NBCUniversal from General Electric and later, AT&T Broadband in 2011.

In addition to his successful advocacy on behalf of his employer, Earle has built a reputation for helping to develop the next generation of industry leaders. He has been a mentor to his colleagues and also serves on the Congressional Black Caucus Foundation and secretary to CBCF executive board, a nonprofit research organization working to train future leaders and to advance community awareness and public policies affecting African Americans.

One of my favorite presidents, Teddy Roosevelt, is famously quoted as saying, "Speak softly and carry a big stick; you will go far." Without question, Earle carries a big stick representing Comcast, one of the nation's largest cable, Internet, and telephone providers. Fortunately, the company has chosen wisely in entrusting such responsibility with Earle, who, with his soft-spoken manner, has helped skillfully advance the agenda of Comcast and the telecommunications industry as a whole.

Gerry Connolly
Member of Congress

EARLE JONES—TELECOM POLICY EXTRAORDINAIRE
By Congressman G. K. Butterfield (North Carolina's 1st district)

I have had the high honor of knowing and working with Earle Jones over the past decade. As a member of Congress, I have many relationships on Capitol Hill, but none exceed the bond of friendship that I enjoy with Earle Jones. Earle is one of the kindest individuals I've ever come to know.

Earle doesn't just stop by my office when he needs something like so many whose job it is to advocate on behalf of their company's interests. Sometimes he drops by just to say hello. Whatever the reason for his visits, you know it's Earle the second he walks in the door; his deep voice and commanding presence fill the room.

I've always been impressed by Earle's honesty and integrity. He knows what he knows, but maybe more importantly, he also knows what he doesn't know. That's exceedingly rare in Washington. His ability to break down complex policy issues into something that is easily understood is one of his many great talents. His tremendous advocacy for the advancement of African Americans is another.

Earle has generously given his time to serve on the Congressional Black Caucus Foundation Corporate Advisory Council where he advised the CBCF's board of directors on policy, special initiatives, and leadership development. There is no doubt that Earle's service on the council furthered CBCF's mission to advance the global black community by developing leaders, informing policy, and educating the public. His professional drive is matched by his love for family.

Earle has traced his wife's, Linda, family roots to my congressional district in Winton, North Carolina. A descendant of Frazier and Flora Newsome Mitchell, Linda embraces and covets the legacy of her wonderful ancestors. Each generation that followed Frazier and Flora used the examples of those that preceded them, resulting in accomplishments that are too numerous to recite.

Earle's steadfast leadership and dogged commitment to always exemplify things the right way and not the easy way has enabled him to earn the trust and respect of his friends, colleagues, congressional staffers, and countless members of Congress. Like so many others, I am honored to know Earle Jones and call him my friend.

G. K. Butterfield
Member of Congress

COMMUNICATING EXCELLENCE
By Congressman Alcee L. Hastings (Florida's 20th district)

It has been my distinct honor to work with and get to know Earle Jones. Earle is an effective leader, well respected in his field, and an outstanding representative for Comcast.

Through his work with the Congressional Black Caucus Foundation (CBCF) and Comcast, Earle has continuously achieved significant results. He played an instrumental role in Comcast/General Electric's acquisition of NBCUniversal and continues to provide expert information on the telecommunications industry. I want to congratulate him on his recent appointment as an officer of the CBCF's board of directors and look forward to working with him in that capacity.

In getting to know Earle over the years, I have seen firsthand the important and valuable work that he has done for the African American community and for this nation. I am proud to call Earle my friend and wish him much continued success in the future.

Alcee Hastings
Member of Congress

A REAL GOOD MAN
By Congressman James Clyburn (South Carolina's 6th district)

I've known Earle Jones for many years. During those years, we have shared more early-morning breakfasts than either of our ages will allow us to remember. He's a good man, and I'm proud to call him my friend.

James Clyburn
Member of Congress

PERSONAL
BUSINESS
RELATIONSHIPS

"Treasure your relationships, not your possessions."
—Anthony J. D'Angelo

Another window into how Earle views relationships is the manner in which he embraces and preserves the relationships he has with those providing various business services to him and family: purchase and maintenance of vehicles, hair care, cleaners, banking, medical, physical fitness, financial investments, home mortgages, purchase of clothing, house maintenance, florist, pharmacy, and so on. They all know "Mr. Jones." He has dealt with most of these business providers for over 25 years.

On occasion, if I have to drop off or pick up some clothes from the cleaners, the very first thing they ask me is "Where's Mr. Jones, is he out of town?" I know today many businesses will provide home delivery and pickup service—well, Mr. Jones had that before it became fashionable because he was such a valued customer of the businesses he frequented. The providers love his temperament, his caring, patient, and courteous manner (to people that generally receive neutral, at best, treatment from customers). They tell me how Mr. Jones treats them or that his responses make a difference in their day. Earle has been very fortunate because many staff persons at the businesses he frequents have been there for many years. Even when staff turns over, the new relationships develop very quickly.

Other family members and friends benefit from the relationships Earle established over the years. Our son still goes to the same cleaners, hair care salon, car dealership and maintenance shop, and mortgage broker. Because Earle values these relationships, he is very selective in any personal references he will make to these businesses.

To provide some insight into the depth of these relationships, Earle has only purchased cars from two car dealerships in Fairfax County over the past 25 years. Like most families with multiple drives, we have multiple cars, and if the dealerships that Earle had the relationships with didn't have the car or could not get it, we did not get the car. However, we never had a problem in that area because "Mr. Jones's" relationships were always very deep. The owner's son of a very large dealership in the metro area actually delivered a car to our house that the dealership owner got from an automobile sale outside of the area. Earle has actually purchased over 12 cars or SUVs from that dealership. He definitely has a large file there.

However, if the service is not or does not stay at par, Earle will sever those relationships, with everyone knowing where the breakdown lies. Earle has never been viewed as unreasonable in his expectations for quality service and expedited business transitions by those who deal with him. That is one of the reasons they work so hard to maintain his business. He is faithful.

PERSONAL BUSINESS ESSAYS

- **Alison Lucas**, General Sales Manager, Ted Britt Ford

- **Mario Majano**, Manager, Crest Cleaners

- **Edric McSween**, CRPC, Financial Planner, Ameriprise Financial Services Inc.

- **Dora Merino**, Owner, Doris Cleaning Services

- **Antonio Palacios**, Assistant Manager, Crest Cleaners

- **Manya Rayner**, President and CEO, Churchill Mortgage

- **Ron West**, President and CEO, Rush Fitness, LLC

SALT OF THE EARTH

In my 54 years, I have met only a few people that I really admire. Earle Jones is one of those few people. I have been fortunate to know him both professionally and personally. Only Earle begins a business voice mail with "This is Earle Jones. I hope all is well with you and your family . . ." AND he says it with complete sincerity. Even during intense business negotiations, I have never heard him raise his voice or speak crossly. My husband, Ray, and I have known Linda and Earle for many years and treasure them as people we know we could count on to help us if we needed it.

Ray and Earle are similar in that they tend to be quiet men of few words, but are thought-provoking when they speak. I told Ray that I had so many things to say about Earle and was trying to find the perfect words. As the men often do for Linda and me, he came up with these words for Earle that describe him perfectly.

"Earle is a considerate, thoughtful, cerebral person
who handles himself like a true gentleman at all times."

What a legacy!

I couldn't have said it better myself—not in one sentence. So, I thought about what would be the one word that best describes Earle. I thought long and hard, and ultimately, it was a tie between kind, gentle, intelligent, godly, respectful, strong, witty, caring, passionate, and "salt of the earth." I absolutely could not choose one above the other. So, I decided the only word that exemplifies all of these qualities to me is simply . . . "Earle."

WE LOVE YOU, EARLE!
Manya and Ray Rayner

SUPERMAN-IN-WAITING

I've had the pleasure of working with Earle as his personal trainer for the past few years. When we first started, he had a weak shoulder. As one of his primary goals of getting in shape, it's been awesome to see him get stronger and stronger each day.

In turn, through weight training and conditioning, he has strengthened his shoulder and entire body greatly. Earle's least favorite exercise is running five flights of stairs. Every time I say to him, "Let's hit the stairs, you've got this," he says, "Come on, Ron" but always gives it 100 percent.

He's always very aware of my time demands. He's on time and ready to start the workout. He lets me know ahead of time if his travel schedule will conflict with the workout ahead of time so we can reschedule the time based on my schedule. How courteous and heartfelt.

Earle is more than a client. He's a friend. During our training sessions, I look forward to our conversations. Although Earle may appear to be quiet and reserved, I learned that he is well connected and respected by his family, colleagues, and associates. His roots run deep. He is well traveled, and his conversation reflects that without boasting, just a matter-of-fact way of adding information to a conversation to educate. He loves his family and often speaks of his wife, Linda, and grandkids.

During my difficult time losing my mother recently, Earle was one of the friends I felt at ease talking to—it was obvious he is a caring man and showed compassion for my situation.

It's a pleasure training Earle, and I treasure our continued friendship and watching him evolve into SUPERMAN—the cape is waiting, Earle.

Ron West
President and CEO
RUSH Fitness, LLC

THE BIG GUY WITH THE BIG SMILE

I have had the pleasure of working for Earle and Linda for over 15 years, providing cleaning services for their home in Vienna. Even though we see Linda more than Earle, when he is around, he always has a big welcoming smile on his face. He always speaks and asks how we're doing. My cleaning ladies think he is so handsome, too.

I have many professional clients that live in the same area as Earle and Linda. Without a doubt few are as caring as Earle. He wants to make sure we are "OK" and language is not a problem because he listens with his heart. If something goes wrong, he never seems to be angry; he is so calm trying to understand.

He is a great person to work for. We have helped out on many occasions with parties and other events they have had at their home. Earle worries about the ladies getting home or staying late because he knows they have small children. If Earle and Linda need help putting up or taking down Christmas decorations or extra cleaning, my ladies are always eager to work extra time at their home. We have trust in him, and he has our unlimited trust and support. We take care of their home as if were ours.

We consider Earle and Linda like family because they treat us like family. They live their Christian values every day. They say the measure of a man is more about how he treats people who cannot do anything for him. Earle Jones treats us with respect and dignity, which sometimes is hard to find in our business.

Dora Merino, Owner
Doris Cleaning Services

"OLD SCHOOL"

In life, each day is an opportunity to grow and expand our minds. I lived in New York for the first 40 years of my life, and it was during that 40 years I was able to confidently discern the positives and negatives to guide me in the universe. When I moved to the Maryland, Virginia, and District area to build my financial planning practice in 1992, I relied on this instinct to find likeminded individuals with similar values:

- Family First

- Importance of Building and Protecting Wealth

- Integrity and Respect for Others

- Friendship

Seemed simple enough, but today's world is filled with people that have no sense of the importance of these things that should be so commonplace, they are sometimes as far away to reach as the stars and the moon.

About 20 years ago, I met Earle Jones as a referral from Linda to discuss financial planning. Earle, a very well established attorney relocating to the District from Denver, was an extremely interesting and intelligent individual. Not only had Earle realized some interesting professional achievements, but more importantly, he had a strong value system and awareness of the challenges in life as a black man. We started a small reading group with a few who shared similar values, which evolved into a dynamic discussion group. I was able to get to know Earle not only as a business associate but as a friend who embraced so many of the values which are part of me. We evolved from business associates, to reading buddies, to what I feel is today a good friendship built on a solid foundation. That may seem normal, but I have found it rare that often individuals find it difficult to be true over time and to be consistent about their alignment with their life goals. Not Earle. Earle has truly been a model of discipline and consistency, which, in my opinion, is not only necessary, but is Key to Success in Life.

Earle, "Old School," while successful in so many areas of his life—professionally, family, church, and probably too many friends to count—is rooted in those old-school core values which were created by an incredibly sound family training from a child. His respect for others and thoughtfulness are a legacy for all. My friendship with Earle during these last 20 years has had an impact on my personal growth. I call Earle my "old-school" friend because we have traveled a similar spiritual journey and are most fulfilled when we can help others. As we continue our life journey, I am hopeful that the sharing of life's knowledge and compassion for others continues to be a bond that we embrace into eternity.

Edric McSween, CRPC, Financial Planner
Ameriprise Financial Services Inc.

ALWAYS THANKS WITH A SMILE

We got to know Mr. Jones in 2003 under not-so-pleasant circumstances. He dropped his cleaning off, and when he returned to pick the cleaning up, it was not ready. Needless to say, he was not pleased because he was traveling the next day and had planned to take those clothes with him. We apologized profusely and offered not to charge for his cleaning.

We could see Mr. Jones not only accepted our apologies, but he showed some understanding for an honest mistake and continued to come back. Other customers have said things to us that we cannot print here for things far less. He showed compassion, and we respected that and from that visit on—he has become our PREMIER customer.

Mr. Jones always greets us with a smile. He asks, "How's your day going?" and "How are you?" And he really means it. He takes time to exchange pleasantries but will make small conversation about other things that are going on. He never comes in with a rushed or hurried manner—he puts us at ease. Most people are just in and out without even speaking other than saying their name for the cleaning. Most do not acknowledge us when we say thank you.

After 12 years with him coming every week—we think he is AWESOME and love the chocolates he gives us at Christmastime. We get concerned if a week goes by and we do not see him. We even pick up from his house and will deliver, but we think he likes coming in and the personal interactions. We really appreciate the personal interaction because Mr. Jones is one of a kind.

Mario Majano and Antonio Palacios
Crest Cleaners

THE CALM, DEEP, REASSURING VOICE

I've had a business relationship with Earle for over 12 years at Ted Britt Ford in Fairfax, Virginia. When I first met Earle, I was the finance manager for the company. Usually by the time a client gets to me in the purchase of a vehicle, they can be a bit frustrated and sometimes with a short fuse for a time consuming process that's fairly paper intensive. But not Earle!!

He has purchased 10 vehicles since I've worked here and 2 prior to my tenure. Everyone here loves to work with Earle, he is our "gold standard" of clients. Whenever he comes in; patience is what you see, regardless of how busy we are. He takes the time to see past the situation to see the person and from that we quickly move to a place that allows us to focus on what he needs and how we can provide it.

Even though Earle has purchased many vehicles from us , he never uses that as a calling card to make demands of us. He never considers throwing his weight around and this is typically not what you hear from others who have done a lot less business with us.

I've been the General Sales Manager for several years now and Earle has worked with some of the newer sales persons on my staff and they all say, he is so encouraging and respectful of them. During some of the sales transactions, many have told me, his deep, calm and reassuring voice puts them at ease. He's an encourager and the people like that about him; they solicit advice from him and see him as a person with a tremendous amount of humility, integrity and concern for his fellow man.

Everyone here looks forward to seeing Earle when he comes in and I have the pleasure of knowing and working with his wife, Linda, son, Steve and daughter-in-law, Heather and those two beautiful grandkids. Such a beautiful family led by such a great man. Earle is part of the Ted Britt family, too.

Alison Lucas
General Sales Manager
Ted Britt Ford
Fairfax, VA

BOOKS, BOOKS, BOOKS

One cannot know Earle and not be aware of his love for reading and books. Even though the medium today has shifted away from the production and sale of hardcopy books, Earle will read online newspapers, magazines, articles, sports, political commentaries, blogs, etc., but not online books. He maintains it's sacrilege to read a book online, so he still purchases hardcopy books or paperbacks. He averages 1–2 a month, and he reads them. We have a collection of about 3,000 books throughout the house. We have bookcases on every floor of our home, books orderly stacked under end and console tables, inside cabinets, boxes stored in the basement, and, various baskets I have in reading corners. I don't think there is a room without a book. About every 5 years, I go through his "collection" or "libraries,"—with lots of resistance—to donate some books to local charities to maintain a reasonable level of written materials in the house. I've attempted to maintain a bibliography by subject and author, but it became an overwhelming task. We do have some sense of which room a book may be in if you want to borrow one.

Earle's interests are very diverse, so there are not many topics we do not have a book on.He's not very interested in fiction; however, autobiographies and documentaries will catch his eye. He is very interested in African (Egyptian, in particular) history, literature, the state of African American people in the U.S., world civilizations, religion, wealth building and finance, world politics, and sports. Most of the statistical and demographical data on various topics, Earle now gets online.

Just recently, I ran across Earle's Cub Scout and Boy Scout manuals from elementary school, his Orientation to Coolidge High School manual, and several Batman comic books. I decided to save the Batman comic books for his great-nephews or grandson.

The love for books existed when Earle was in elementary school and grew in intensity over his lifetime. His sister and I played a prank on him several summers ago. She found at least two dozen books Earle had checked out of the library when he was in junior high and high school and never returned. We used the library cards and some computer software, and with a little creativity, generated a letter from the District of Columbia library and a bill with penalties and late fees for over $1,750 for the outstanding debt owed the library. At first, he wasn't sure if the letter and bill were true or not; he eventually caught on to our prank. However, Earle was not too surprised he still had the books. Then he started to read the books again.

Earle's love for books, reading, and research with books has provided great examples to others in the family. There is a great appreciation for his knowledge and understanding of the world—past, present, and future, as well as the family history. He continues to maintain and update the family history records using family tree software. If you need to get an answer, he is the Wikipedia of the family. He does this with the same grace and humility as everything else in his life. You never get a lecture, just the facts.

As I was writing this section, I kept thinking about where I should include his extensive knowledge gained through reading various books and sports magazines, now pretty much online, that continues to expand his knowledge on sports. Earle follows college and professional football and basketball to the level he understands intimately the "ins and outs" of the drafts and national championships. His interests extended into the breaking of the color barriers in key sports and positions (like quarterback for Division 1 college and the NFL and NBA professional teams, head coaches, etc.). He follows it as a student of the history being made.

Earle has many books on and quite a reservoir of knowledge of the old Negro baseball league teams during segregation. He reads and keeps up with color barriers being broken in the head coaching and ownership areas as well. I've not seen too many questions directed to him that he could not answer. He keeps up with professional golf, tennis, and boxing. When the Olympics start every 4 years, Earle is quite knowledgeable about the athletes and teams in other countries for the sports he follows.

IN CONCLUSION—THE "EJ" INFLUENCES

When Sam and Nettie Jones, in the 1920s, and later, Earle and Sylvia Jones, in the 1960s, were living the lessons they were teaching, they had an audience—the younger family members. It is always easier to lead by example—the "do as I do rather than do as I say" model. As a student of his grandfather and father, Earle learned that in order to affect the impact or influence of one's behavior on others, one needs the discipline to be consistent in his beliefs and values—you have to live it every day.

In authoring *Touchstone*, I wanted to present aspects of Earle Francis Jones's life story through the eyes of the people who are his audience each and every day—his family, friends, and colleagues, and that includes me. I have learned so much from Earle—he is my Wikipedia for all topics in life—he responds in a calm and reassuring way, regardless of how many times I ask him to "reexplain because I didn't get it" or "can you give me an example?" or "can you say it another way; that doesn't make sense?" He continues to help me through my fog of understanding or misunderstanding.

How do you know if the works you've done, the services you've provided, and the life you've lived influenced others? Your influence can be difficult to see, mainly because it's hard to see yourself. A simple definition of *influence*: the power to change or affect someone or something; the power to cause changes without directly forcing them to happen; a person or thing that affects someone or something in an important way (Merriam-Webster.com).

When I read the essays from Earle's colleagues, family, and friends, they speak to his affect on them or a situation in an important way without forcing anyone or anything. His modesty and humility are one of his greatest touchstones, or equalizers, that allow his influence to yield positive outcomes. In many instances, that same modesty and humility can prevent him from seeing his influence on others.

From the essays, I could see how Earle's values and beliefs he maintains from his family legacy influence the environments he operates in each day. Earle is looked upon as a: calming voice; relationship builder; steady hand; loyal one; mentor; one speaking the truth; honest broker; leader; not comprising his integrity; role model; coolheaded; devoted friend; humble one; hallmark of success, benchmark of sanity, steadfast and trusted one; and so on—in short, a *"TOUCHSTONE."*

Earle does have this uncanny ability to see things from others' perspective, which is demonstrated in the compassion and empathy one sees in him. He's not very quick to judge and will reflect and question his own thoughts and actions in a situation to bring some balance into it. The essays from a very diverse group of people throughout his life bear witness that he does influence their thoughts, actions, and deeds by being the person he is.

The nerd side of me could not see all those similar phrases, nouns, and adjectives across all the essays describing Earle without analyzing them in some mathematical or statistical manner. So, I created a spreadsheet of all the root words (*care* represents *caring* or *cared*, etc.) and phrases that were used across all the essays—then eliminated any root words that were not used 10 times or more across essays to get a manageable statistical sample since the range was 2–355. I ended up with eight clusters represented in the chart below. Very similar to the slices of his life represented in the pie chart in the Introduction.

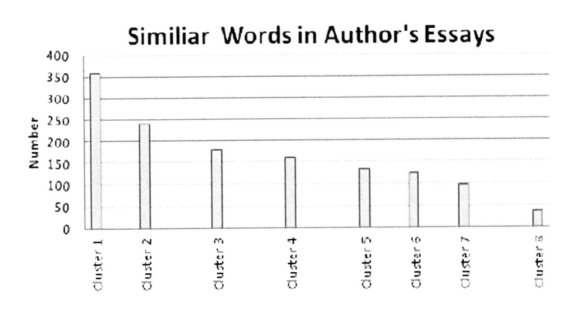

Cluster	Similar Words in Authors Essays	Number
1	Family/ family-oriented, friend, friendship, relationship	355
2	Loving, caring, respectful, supportive, honorable, honest, genuine	239
3	Leader, leadership, successful, strong, courageous, proud, admiration, accomplished, achiever, hallmark of success	180
4	Committed, commitment, education, steadfast/steady, benchmark for reasonableness, trusting, loyal, unselfish, faithful	162
5	Religion, church, blessings	131
6	Service, dedicated, devoted, dependable	123
7	Mentor. mentoring, role model, wisdom, wise, counsel, Influential, inspiring	95
8	Royalty, noble, nobility, gracious	35

What this tells me is how the world sees Earle is pretty much in sync with his personal values and principles he lives each day—passed down to him from that powerful family legacy.

Like his father, Earle believes in the importance of building and protecting your wealth. He feels very strongly about generational wealth and the ability to pass on to the next generations something more than debt, and that includes financial stewardship to your religious institutions or church. Earle recognizes all gifts come from God, and we are the stewards of those gifts, and we have a responsibility to make the best out of what God gives us. This is the kind of financial prudence that always reminds one that it's our responsibility to look after our own family and teach them how to look after their families, and then others—not to be a burden on anyone. However, this belief is balanced within one of the most sensitive, generous, and caring persons you'll meet. Earle believes most of this can be accomplished through prudent financial decision making in one's life. He works extremely hard to ensure that his families on both sides of the Atlantic have sound financial plans and resources. He is that strong shepherd who protects his sheep financially and ensures we are knowledgeable enough to manage our lives financially as well.

Another lesson Earle passes on to others is the politeness and courtesy he shows to women, young ladies, and girls, regardless of age. It is a lesson for females to expect it, and for males to imitate it. He always opens the door for me, whether we are going to a state dinner or to get some ice cream at the shopping center. It's who he is, and I've seen that influence on other young men in our lives mimicking him. It may be old school today, but Earle believes it is a sign of respect and humility.

Earle has withstood the test of time; he is a man of utmost integrity and unflappable grace under pressure with a clear head and solid faith. We all depend on him for these characteristics as they help guide us through some trying times, very similar to the way his grandfather, Sam Jones, guided his family members out of harm's way in Sylvester, Georgia, to safety in Jacksonville, Florida, and then on to a new life in Newtonville, New Jersey.

EARLE F. JONES, WE SALUTE YOU!!!

"TOUCHSTONE"

Lyrics for a Musical Tribute to Earle Jones
Written and Arranged by Joshua Rich

You're always there in times of need
A friend, a giver
And so graciously you lead
You are no ordinary man
A gentle giant, lifting up his fellow man

You are courageous, salt of the earth
Faithful, humble
From the moment of your birth
The biggest little brother you could be
Always taking time to care, so lovingly

Chorus

You're our touchstone
Our lighthouse in a storm
A solid rock of love that greets each dawn
Our touchstone
So steadfast and so strong
The shoulder that we always lean upon

A loving father, a devoted son
You stand up for your convictions
You are second to none
Loyal, educated, true nobility
A traveler, a teacher, and all the world can see

Chorus

Life is what you make it
That is what you've shown
Forging your own pathway,
With seeds that you have sown
A love for books, a joy for music
And all whom you have known
Would say you are like Atlas
With incredible backbone

Instrumental

Sometimes words can't possibly convey
All the things that someone wants to say
And so it is with you—we just can't find
A way to show all the love that we feel inside

Chorus

Helping us to always carry on
Thank God we have our touchstone
This blessed soul we all depend upon

www.joshuarich.com